Vanya and Sonia
and Masha and Spike

Christopher Durang works published by Grove Press:

The Marriage of Bette and Boo

Laughing Wild and *Baby with the Bathwater*

Christopher Durang Explains It All for You
(volume includes:
The Nature and Purpose of the Universe
'dentity Crisis
Titanic
The Actor's Nightmare
Sister Mary Ignatius Explains It All for You
Beyond Therapy)

Betty's Summer Vacation

Miss Witherspoon and *Mrs. Bob Cratchit's Wild Christmas Binge*

Why Torture Is Wrong, and the People Who Love Them
and Other Political Plays

Vanya and Sonia and Masha and Spike

CHRISTOPHER DURANG

Grove Press
New York

Printed in the United States of America
Published simultaneously in Canada

ISBN: 978-0-8021-2238-4
eBook ISBN: 978-0-8021-9272-1

CAUTION: Professionals and amateurs are hereby warned that *Vanya and Sonia and Masha and
Spike* is subject to a royalty. It is fully protected under the copyright laws of the United States,
Canada, United Kingdom, and all British Commonwealth countries, and all countries covered by
the International Copyright Union, the Pan-American Copyright Convention, and the Universal
Copyright Convention. All rights, including professional, amateur, motion picture, recitation, public
reading, radio broadcasting, television, video or sound taping, all other forms of mechanical or
electronic reproduction, such as information storage and retrieval systems and photocopying, and
rights of translation into foreign languages, are strictly reserved.

Stock and amateur applications for permission to perform *Vanya and Sonia and Masha and Spike* must be made
in advance to Dramatists Play Service (440 Park Avenue South, New York, NY 10016, telephone: 212-683-
8960, www.dramatists.com) and by paying the requisite fee, whether the plays are presented for charity or gain
and whether or not admission is charged. First Class and professional applications must be made in advance to
ICM Partners, Attn: Patrick Herold, 730 Fifth Avenue, New York, NY 10019 and by paying the requisite fee.

Grove Press
an imprint of Grove/Atlantic, Inc.
154 West 14th Street
New York, NY 10011

Distributed by Publishers Group West

www.groveatlantic.com

13 14 15 16   10 9 8 7 6 5 4

To my partner of 25 years, John Augustine

INTRODUCTION

by David Hyde Pierce

In May of 2012, I got this note from Christopher Durang:

> *Dear David,*
>
> *I have a new play that is being co-produced in the fall by McCarter Theatre and Lincoln Center. It's called* Vanya and Sonia and Masha and Spike. *It's not a parody; it's set in the present in Bucks County. Vanya and Masha are brother and sister, and Sonia is their adopted sister. They were given those names by their professor parents, who are now dead. But in some ways they do resemble Chekhov characters. I like to say the play takes Chekhovian characters and themes and puts them in a blender. The play is funny, but has genuine emotion in it as well. Nicky Martin is to direct. Sigourney W will be Masha, Kristine Nielsen, Sonia.*

Chris asked if I would read the play, and if I would play Vanya, and I did both those things, and I'm so glad I did. It's a very funny play, and a field day for the actors in all six roles. It is also richly layered, and its odd mix of contemporary references with Chekhovian themes and language creates a uniquely Durangian world.

The opening is a good example of what I'm talking about. It takes place in the morning room of a country house—a very Chekhovian setting, though this happens to be in Pennsylvania:

SONIA I brought you coffee, dearest Vanya.

VANYA I have some.

SONIA Oh. But I bring you coffee every morning.

VANYA Well, yes, but you weren't available.

SONIA Well, I was briefly in the bathroom, you couldn't wait?

The first line could be straight from Chekhov, the last line definitely isn't. In five lines Chris reveals the relationship between the siblings, and establishes the world of the play. I read those lines, and I was hooked.

Chris actually wrote the character of Masha for his longtime pal and collaborator Sigourney Weaver, and he wrote Sonia for Kristine Nielsen, another dear friend and a veteran of Chris's plays. I mention this so you'll know, as you read, that the voices and the style of performance weren't exaggerated or extreme—the roles were played by actors who inhabited them easily. The younger actors—Billy Magnussen, Shalita Grant, and Genevieve Angelson—were, to quote Masha, "pretty and luminous and full of youthful hope and enthusiasm." They were also very gifted and highly skilled, and played their characters as people, not caricatures.

Rehearsals with our great director Nicholas Martin began at the McCarter Theatre in Princeton, New Jersey, and that turned out to be a wonderful bonding experience. Most of us lived in Manhattan, so we'd pile into cars, or train back and forth together. Once the play opened we'd stay over in Princeton, drinking after the show at night, going for a run or taking odd field trips during the day. In Act II Vanya mentions watching the movie *Old Yeller* as a child—Sigourney and Kristine and I watched it one night in my apartment, huddled together on the sofa, crying our eyes out. That bonding continued as we moved from Princeton to Lincoln Center and then to Broadway; audience members said the closeness of the company was palpable in performance. That might be worth remembering as you read—for all the fighting and jealousy and sibling rivalry in the play, there is much love between these characters, as there was between the actors who first played them.

Chris originally wrote the role of Vanya for himself (Chris is an actor as well), and the character is in many ways a quiet observer throughout most of the play. He is also a peacemaker, which I think Chris may have been at certain times in his own family. But like Chekhov's Uncle Vanya, this Vanya finally gets a chance to express himself. I don't want to tell you too much about it, I hate when introductions give away what happens. However, I will say that when we had the first reading of the play, I started into that part, which I'd just thought of as funny and angry, and in the midst of it I became very emotional, which came as a surprise to me and everyone else. Apparently Chris had tapped into something, and as we moved from rehearsals to performance, we found the audiences thought so too.

Whatever that something is, I don't want to name it. It has roots in the lighter, playful-seeming first act, and it blossoms in the fight, the phone call, the rant and the revelations of Act II. There are themes in the play—changes in the climate and in life, the loss of personal connection, the insanity of popular culture—that were particularly relevant to our audiences, and many people said that Chris articulated things they were thinking but hadn't spoken. Like Chekhov before him, Chris has written a very particular comedy about very specific people, yet in the process he has touched on something universal.

One last thing: In the play, Vanya is worried about climate change and global warming and whether the planet ultimately would survive. A few times during the run we had to temporarily cut or change lines about the weather, because some actual natural disaster had happened, and what had been a funny exaggeration in the play was no longer funny or an exaggeration. (Chris can be Cassandra-like in his ability to predict what's about to happen in the world.)

If you're reading this, then the world hasn't come to an end. But if it's about to, and you've chosen to spend your last minutes reading *Vanya and Sonia and Masha and Spike,* then good for you. What a way to go.

May 12, 2013

Hi, Everyone,

I am delighted to be here with all of you to award the New York Drama Critics' Circle's Best Play of 2013 to this playwright I've kind of heard of—Christopher Durang. It is an inspired and thrilling choice. I went online to see who else had won this very prestigious award, and the list is dazzling ... monumental writers who created our cultural landscape and are the reason many of us fell in love with the theater in the first place: O'Neill, Williams, Inge, Miller, Guare, Albee, Stoppard, Wilson, Vogel, Wasserstein, and now there at the end is Chris's name for *Vanya and Sonia and Masha and Spike*, and it looks so right there.

And if I may—there are not too many laugh-out-loud comedies on this list. *Rosencrantz and Guildenstern*—okay. Neil Simon won once for *Brighton Beach Memoirs*, but I can't remember if that's one of his funny plays. And certainly there is no mention from the old days of Kaufman and Hart, or the great Thornton Wilder, with whom Durang shares a kinship. Imagine how Wilder would have enjoyed Miss Witherspoon!

Comedy is often dismissed as the lesser genre. Of course it's actually more difficult to write a great comedy. As Chris mentioned in an interview—in 1959 the film *Some Like It Hot* received no Oscar nominations while *Ben-Hur* won eleven Academy Awards. And which one would you rather see today?

Molière was derided as a sketch writer because of his love for commedia dell 'arte. But I don't see a lot of Corneille and Racine being done these days, and Moliere is packing people into theaters all over the world.

Chris writes about things that matter deeply to him. And I must tell you that we have so many young people, from teens to twentysomethings, for whom Durang is it. He speaks for them as well as for all of us who remember the happy tedium of licking stamps and dialing a telephone.

So I am delighted that you have recognized the substance, the relevance, and the craftsmanship of *Vanya and Sonia and Masha and Spike*, in spite of the fact that the play is an unabashed crowd pleaser, playing nightly to ecstatic sold-out crowds who have only one complaint—that their faces ache from laughing so much even as they are crying their hearts out. It is recognition not only well-deserved but long overdue.

I am enormously proud to present the New York Drama Critics' Circle Award for Best Play of 2013, for *Vanya and Sonia and Masha and Spike*, to the prodigiously talented Christopher Durang.

*Vanya and Sonia
and Masha and Spike*

PRODUCTION CREDITS

Vanya and Sonia and Masha and Spike was commissioned by **McCarter Theatre Center** in Princeton, New Jersey and received its world premiere with previews beginning on September 7, 2012, and opening on September 14, 2012. Emily Mann, Artistic Director; Timothy J. Shields, Managing Director; Mara Isaacs, Producing Director. The production was directed by Nicholas Martin; scenic design by David Korins, costume design by Emily Rebholz, lighting design by Justin Townsend, original music and sound design by Mark Bennett, casting by Daniel Swee, assistant director was Bryan Hunt; the production stage manager was Cheryl Mintz. Director of Production was David York, Literary Director was Carrie Hughes, Associate Producer was Adam Immerwahr. McCarter Theatre Center coproduced the production with Lincoln Center Theater.

Vanya and Sonia and Masha and Spike received its New York City premiere at **Lincoln Center Theater** with previews beginning on October 25, 2012, and opening on November 12, 2012. Andre Bishop, Artistic Director; Bernard Gersten, Executive Producer; Adam Siegel, Managing Director in association with McCarter Theatre Center with previews beginning on October 25, 2012, and opened on November 12, 2012. The production was directed by Nicholas Martin; scenic design by David Korins, costume design by Emily Rebholz, lighting design by Justin Townsend, original music and sound design by Mark Bennett, casting by Daniel Swee; the dramaturg was Anne Cattaneo, and the stage manager was Jane Grey.

Vanya and Sonia and Masha and Spike moved to Broadway and played at the **Golden Theatre** in New York City with previews beginning on beginning on March 5, 2013, and opening on March 14, 2013. The play was produced by Joey Parnes, Larry Hirschhorn, and Joan Raffe/Jhett Tolentino, Martin Platt & David Elliott, Pat Flicker Addiss, Catherine Adler, John O'Boyle, Joshua Goodman, Jamie deRoy/Richard Winkler, Cricket Hooper Jiranek/Michael Palitz, Mark S. Golub & David S.

Golub, Radio Mouse Entertainment, Shawdowcatcher Entertainment, Mary Cossette/Barbara Manocherian, Megan Savage/Meredith Lynsey Schade, Hugh Hysell/Richard Jordan, Cheryl Wiesenfeld/Ron Simons, S. D. Wagner, and John Johnson, in association with McCarter Theatre Center and Lincoln Center Theater.

The production was directed by Nicholas Martin, scenic design by David Korins, costume design by Emily Rebholz, lighting design by Justin Townsend, original music and sound design by Mark Bennett, casting by Daniel Swee; the production stage manager was Denise Yaney, the stage manager was M. A. Howard, and the assistant director was Bryan Hunt.

The cast for all three productions was as follows (in order of appearance):

Vanya	David Hyde Pierce
Sonia	Kristine Nielsen
Cassandra	Shalita Grant
Masha	Sigourney Weaver
Spike	Billy Magnussen
Nina	Genevieve Angelson

Understudies: Keith Reddin (Vanya), Linda Marie Larson (Sonia, Masha), Heather Alicia Simms (Cassandra), Creed Garnick (Spike), Liesel Allen Yeager (Nina). (Miss Yeager played the role of Nina for part of the run.)

CHARACTERS

VANYA
50s, living in Bucks County. Resigned to his life, more or less, at least compared to Sonia.

SONIA
His adopted sister, early 50s, living with him in Bucks County. Discontent, upset, regretful.

MASHA
His sister, 50s, glamorous and successful actress who goes gallivanting around the world.

SPIKE
An aspiring actor, 29 or younger, sexy, self-absorbed, Masha's new companion.

NINA
Lovely, sincere would-be actress, early 20s, visiting her aunt and uncle next door. Starstruck and energetic.

CASSANDRA
Cleaning lady and soothsayer, any age, any race. In the original production, she was played by an African American actress in her late 20s.

Set in the present, a lovely farmhouse in Bucks County.

ACT I

A farmhouse in Bucks County, PA. Not enormous, but comfortable, on a hill, many trees, a barn nearby, a pond in the near distance. There used to be a shed for peacocks, but the peacocks are long gone.

The Morning Room. Sunny, a sitting place with a nice window and comfortable wicker chairs.

VANYA, 55 to 60, in a nightshirt, walks in, carrying coffee. He sits, staring out the window. Sips the coffee, which tastes good. He feels somewhat contented. He stares a bit more. SONIA enters, age 50 or so, with coffee for him. Perhaps has a diet soda for herself. She is unsure of herself, melancholy, though keeps hoping for impossible things.

SONIA I brought you coffee, dearest Vanya.

VANYA I have some.

SONIA Oh. But I bring you coffee every morning.

VANYA Well, yes, but you weren't available.

SONIA Well, I was briefly in the bathroom, you couldn't wait?

VANYA I don't know. The coffee was made, you weren't there, I'm capable of pouring coffee into a cup.

SONIA But I like bringing you coffee in the morning.

VANYA Fine. Here, take this cup and give me that one.

SONIA All right.

She hands him the coffee she's brought; he hands her his partly finished cup.

SONIA Now I feel better.

VANYA I'm glad.

7

Sonia sits. They both look out, staring into the distance.

SONIA Has the blue heron been at the pond yet this morning?

VANYA Not yet. Or it was here before I was.

SONIA It'll probably come later. It's such a beautiful bird.

VANYA Yes, it is. (*sips the coffee*) I'm afraid the other cup tasted better.

SONIA Well it's the same coffee.

VANYA Well maybe I put in more milk than you did. Maybe that's why it tastes better.

SONIA Don't I usually put in the right amount of milk?

VANYA Well, yes. I don't usually think about it. It's just that I was drinking one coffee, and liking it, and then suddenly there's a different cup of coffee, and I'm liking it slightly less. It's no big deal. I'm just making pleasant conversation.

SONIA That's not making pleasant conversation. It's first thing in the morning, and you're implying I don't do anything right.

VANYA I didn't say that.

SONIA Yes, you did.

VANYA I didn't.

SONIA Well you implied it.

VANYA Forget it! The coffee's delicious, I love it!

SONIA Oh, for God's sake. Here, take the original cup back.

VANYA No, no, it's not that different. I'm sorry I said anything.

Sonia forces him to take his original coffee cup back, the one he preferred. She takes the second cup back herself.

SONIA I mean I have two pleasant moments every day in my fucking life, and one of them is bringing you coffee.

8

VANYA Sonia, I'm sorry I said anything. Really, the two cups are almost identical. I should have said nothing.

SONIA All right.

VANYA I'm sorry. Really.

SONIA That's all right.

She suddenly takes the cup she's holding and smashes it on the floor, in the direction of the kitchen. Silence.

VANYA Is this how you're going to be today?

SONIA I don't know what you mean.

VANYA YOU JUST THREW THE FUCKING COFFEE AGAINST THE WALL!

SONIA I DIDN'T!

VANYA You didn't??? What kind of idiot response is that?

SONIA I don't know. It's an angry "I hate my life and I hate you" response.

VANYA Well, it was effective then, good for you!

SONIA Thank you!

Silence.

SONIA I'm sorry. I shouldn't have thrown the cup.

VANYA That's all right.

SONIA It's just I had bad dreams last night.

VANYA Oh?

SONIA I dreamt I was 52 and I wasn't married.

VANYA Were you dreaming in the documentary form?

SONIA That's not funny.

VANYA Really, I thought it was. You are 52, and you're not married.

SONIA Whose fault is that?

VANYA Is the answer supposed to be me?

SONIA There isn't any answer. And if I pine for you, that's my business.

VANYA Don't pine for me. That's ridiculous. I'm 57 and I've told you for many years, I'm not interested in you in that way. I . . . march to a different drummer.

SONIA Why must you march to a drummer at all? Why couldn't we both . . . walk to the sounds of a piccolo?

VANYA What? I don't know what that metaphor means. Besides, you're my sister.

SONIA We're not blood relations. I am your adopted sister. So I can pine if I want to.

VANYA Look, I think your pining after me is a tired reflex. I don't think you even like me anymore.

SONIA I agree with you. It's a reflex with me now. It comes from our living together. There's no one else in the house. Ever since Mother and Father died. And Masha left me and you to take care of them while she was off gallivanting, having a life. Don't you feel angry at Masha, that she's had a life?

VANYA Yes, I do. But it's too late now to do anything about it. I must say, I always admired you for doing your duty and taking care of our elderly parents, even though you were adopted. You put Masha to shame, in my opinion.

SONIA Thank you, I appreciate that.

VANYA Of course she had a successful acting career, and you basically didn't have anything *else* to do.

SONIA Well, a moment ago you gave me a lovely compliment. And now . . . oh let's not talk. I'll keep my sadness to myself.

VANYA All right, you do that.

Brief silence. After a while she sighs very heavily, once, twice, maybe three times. Vanya ignores it for a while, but then doesn't.

VANYA Your sadness is very heavy this morning, Sonia. Can you lighten it any?

SONIA No.

VANYA Could you go to a different room?

SONIA Leave the morning room? But I'm in mourning for my life.

VANYA I hope you're not going to make Chekhov references all day.

SONIA If they come up, I may.

VANYA It's been our cross to bear that our parents gave us names from Chekhov plays. The other children made such fun of us with our mysterious names. Such was the burden of having two professor parents; and so active in community theater as well. Remember how good they were in *The Reluctant Debutante*? I don't think they were very good in the *Oresteia*, though, did you?

SONIA No. But I don't think community theater should do Greek tragedy.

VANYA I don't either. Having professors for parents had its drawbacks. Father was so angry when you didn't know something. But what 7-year-old knows who wrote *The Imaginary Invalid*? Father became so enraged when I said Neil Simon. I mean, I was 7.

SONIA And they were very, very difficult once they went mental in old age. Oh but when they were young, how wonderful our parents were, don't you think? Mother was so elegant. And Father showed affection for me often; he called me his little artichoke.

VANYA And he liked artichokes. So it was probably a nice thing he called you that.

SONIA Yes, I think so. And he never molested me.

VANYA That's nice.

SONIA God knows who my actual parents were. I have a feeling they were two drunken Irish people who left me alone every night while they went to the pub. Until one night they were so bombed out of their minds, they walked off a cliff.

VANYA Do you have any *nice* fantasies of who your parents were?

SONIA No.

VANYA I see. (*sips the coffee*) This has gone quite cold now.

SONIA You're just determined to fight over the coffee, aren't you?

VANYA No, I'm really not. I'm debating whether to go microwave the coffee.

SONIA Do you want me to do it?

VANYA Would you? That would be very nice of you.

He hands her the cup. She seems calm but all of a sudden she smashes the cup onto the floor, near where the other one was smashed.

VANYA What is the matter with you???

SONIA Do I have to do everything?

VANYA But you offered to take it. Are you bipolar now?

SONIA Yes!

VANYA Some people claim antidepressants help them.

SONIA If everyone took antidepressants, Chekhov would have had nothing to write about.

VANYA I'm not going to clean up the broken cups, you know.

SONIA Me neither.

VANYA Well, obviously there's no solution.

SONIA The housekeeper comes today. We'll ask her to clean it up.

VANYA What if she refuses?

SONIA We'll fire her.

VANYA All right. We'll never ever pick the cups up, and instead we'll sell the house.

SONIA You can't sell it. You don't own it. Masha owns it.

VANYA I know Masha owns it! But if we leave broken cups and coffee smells all over the house, I'm sure she'll decide she *has* to sell it. And you and I can finally live separately since we hate each other.

SONIA What a good idea!

VANYA A very good idea!

Short pause. They both look out, where presumably there is a picture window.

VANYA It's comforting to have a pond to look at, isn't it? Pretty.

SONIA Yes. I hope the blue heron comes later.

VANYA I hope so too. It's like a good omen.

SONIA Of course, it eats frogs, so it's not a good omen for them.

VANYA No. Nature is cruel. But pretty. And for some reason I think of the blue heron as a harbinger of good luck.

Enter CASSANDRA. *She's 30-60, dressed comfortably for cleaning. Or maybe a colorful dress, an exotic style, something she actually looks good in.*

CASSANDRA Beware the ides of March!

VANYA What?

CASSANDRA Beware the ides of March!

SONIA March? Isn't it late August?

CASSANDRA Beware the middle of the month! Beware of Greeks bearing gifts!

Suddenly she feels inspiration from above, or from somewhere—her psychic powers suddenly turn on, maybe her head moves, or her eyes flutter; she is visited by visions/thoughts, and what she says she dramatically intones, sounding a bit like a speech in Greek tragedy. We should hear her words, she should make sense of them, but they should also be said fast, her mind and psyche are receiving thoughts quickly.

O wretches!
into the Land of Darkness we sail
in a pea green boat;
all around us is full of fire,
and the Delaware River overflows its bank,
and dismal moans rise from Bucks County,
where amity and enmity intermingle.
Portents of dismay
and calamity
yawn beneath the yonder cliff.
O fools looking behind but not looking ahead,
Dost thou not sense thy attendant doom?

VANYA Cassandra, I have asked you repeatedly to please just say "good morning." All right?

CASSANDRA I see visions. Shadows of what lies ahead. It is my curse to see these shadows and my duty to warn you.

VANYA Cassandra, I think you take your name too seriously.

CASSANDRA My name? What do you mean?

VANYA You know. Greek mythology. Apollo gave Cassandra second sight, but then cursed her so no one ever believed her.

CASSANDRA Oh I know that. (*sudden psychic thought pops into her head*) Oh my God! I see something imminent. It's going to happen any moment. One of you is going to take two cups of coffee, and smash them onto the floor. (*she looks between them*) It will be you, Vanya. Don't do it!

SONIA It already happened.

14

CASSANDRA Then I was right!

SONIA No, you said it was GOING to happen, and it already has happened.

CASSANDRA But I am correct you will want me to clean it up. Right? Where are the broken cups?

SONIA (*pointing*) Right over there.

CASSANDRA (*looks*) Oh my God! I was right. You did this, you, Vanya, broke the cups.

SONIA That's right, he did.

VANYA Just clean it up, would you please?

SONIA Clean it up, clean it up!!!

CASSANDRA Fie on you both! I see doom and destruction swirling around you.

VANYA No, just say good morning. Try it.

CASSANDRA Good morning.

VANYA Thank you. Good morning.

SONIA Good morning.

CASSANDRA And yet, what's good about it? Beware of Hootie Pie.

SONIA Who?

CASSANDRA I don't know. Just beware of her. Or it.

VANYA Hootie Pie. We need to keep a small notebook nearby and write all these things down. For your sanity hearing later.

SONIA Hootie Pie. Is that a first name, "Hootie Pie"? Or is "Hootie" the first name, and "Pie" the last name?

VANYA Or maybe Hootie Pie is a pie. And you can order it at a restaurant.

CASSANDRA I don't know what Hootie Pie is. I just know you must beware it.

She feels another psychic message. Maybe her head moves or maybe her eyes flutter. Something.

And also beware of something happening to this house. (*walks toward them, or walks in a bit of a circle*) The house, beware. Be wary. Something bad is coming. You may lose the house.

VANYA Lose it?

CASSANDRA Someone will sell the house right from under you and you will become homeless. You will walk many miles to the poorhouse.

SONIA Surely someone would give us a ride.

CASSANDRA No, you will walk.

VANYA And I don't think there are such things as the poorhouse anymore.

CASSANDRA You will live in the gutter then. Excuse me, I must go and get a Dust Buster and a pail of water and sponge to CLEAN UP YOUR MESS!

She exits, angry.

VANYA I wish she wouldn't come every week and tell us terrible things. It feels abusive.

SONIA Yes, but sometimes she seems to get some of it right, no? Remember when she said a bat was going to get inside the house, and then it did at 2 a.m.

VANYA Yes, true.

SONIA Or that time she said I was going to break my middle toe, and minutes later I did.

VANYA Yes, but that may have been some kind of hypnotic suggestion.

SONIA Nonetheless she said those things and they happened. And when she started to talk about our losing the house, the house where we've been so happy, I became sad, and frightened.

VANYA Where we've been so happy?

SONIA I know I complain, but in some ways I love it here. It's where I've been since I was 8 years old. I came from an orphanage, into a family that either loved me or pretended to, I get confused about that. And it's pretty here. And I love to look at the pond. I love the wild turkeys who wander about the property, I like learning they're so awkward that they sleep in trees but repeatedly fall out of them. I identify with them. I often fall out of my bed, thrashing about in my restless sleep. I am a wild turkey. I am a wild turkey. And I love the cherry orchard in the spring. All the pink blossoms, nature so resplendent.

VANYA The cherry orchard? What cherry orchard?

SONIA We have 10 or 11 cherry trees, they blossom every spring. Do you not remember?

VANYA I remember. But it's not an orchard. You don't call 10 or 11 trees an orchard.

SONIA I do. I wouldn't call 2 or 3 trees an orchard, but 10 or 11 trees, I do call an orchard.

Cassandra comes back with a Dust Buster, and cleans up the broken pieces of cups . . .

CASSANDRA Beware of chicken with salmonella. Beware of mushrooms that grow in the meadow.

SONIA Just clean up the floor, would you? And besides your entreaties never tell us what to do to protect ourselves.

CASSANDRA Beware of thinking too much! Focus on the little things. One foot after another. Enjoying a good cup of coffee and not smashing it onto the ground. A lovely chocolate cookie.

17

VANYA Oh I'd like a cookie.

SONIA I would too.

VANYA Oh remember when Nana used to bring us tea and graham crackers to tide us over until dinner.

SONIA Oh, graham crackers, graham crackers!

VANYA And Masha would never have more than one . . . she was preparing to be an actress even then, and chose to watch her figure.

SONIA Imagine eating only one graham cracker. (*suddenly remembering*) Oh, Masha! I forgot to tell you. She's coming out here today.

VANYA Masha is coming? She called?

SONIA I forgot to tell you.

VANYA No, you purposely don't tell me things. It's one of the ways in which you make life unnecessarily complicated.

SONIA (*angry, feeling criticized*) I FORGOT to tell you. I am bi-polar and I have incipient dementia.

VANYA What time is she coming?

SONIA In an hour or so.

Suddenly there is the sound of a car pulling up outside.

SONIA No . . . sooner.

Vanya realizes he's in his nightshirt, and goes quickly upstairs, or maybe toward the kitchen, in order to pull on pants.

CASSANDRA (*referring to the car outside*) Beware of Greeks bearing gifts. A Trojan horse can hide many things. Someone is with your sister, and he carries Trojans in his back pocket. I will be in the basement doing laundry. If I hear gunshots, I'll come back up.

Cassandra exits.

18

SONIA I really think we should get a new cleaning woman.

Vanya returns with pants. He lets the top of the nightshirt pass as a regular shirt.

VANYA Why is Masha here? Did she say?

Enter MASHA, attractive and grand, mid 50s, and looking great. With her is a handsome young man named SPIKE, age 27 or so. Spike is maybe dressed in worn-out jeans with rips in them. Or maybe is wearing more trendy, relaxed clothes. Sure of himself, and self-involved. Also outgoing.

Masha is dressed well, a bit glamorous as if she might run into photographers somewhere.

MASHA Dearest Vanya. Sweetest Sonia. How wonderful to see you. How I've missed you, and this beautiful house. (*realizes she's missing something*) Spike, darling, would you go to the car? I forgot to bring my Snow White costume.

SPIKE Okay.

MASHA And don't forget the shepherd's crook.

SPIKE Okay. (*to Vanya and Sonia, friendly, wised-up*) Women, huh?

Spike exits.

MASHA Sweetest Vanya, dearest Sonia. How I've missed you. You both look the same. Older. Sadder. But the same. It's wonderful to see you, Vanya. Oh, and you too, Sonia.

SONIA Yes, hello. I'm easy to miss.

MASHA You are! I often miss you! I'm in a play or a movie, and I think of my dear Sonia, and think, oh I miss her! I must call her. Then I get called to the set and months go by and I forget to call. Life happens, no?

SONIA Not here it doesn't. We sit still a lot. We look out the window. We bicker. We long for what the world cannot give. We are in our twilight years, and we realize we have never really lived.

MASHA (*lightly*)   Oh, that's too bad.. (*back to herself, happy*) Oh I wish I had time to sit still. I'm always busy, I'm always on the TV, or flying off to some foreign country to make a movie. Oh I wish I had time to read the classics, sit in a chair, and just read. Do you read the classics, Sonia?

SONIA   No. I think of it, but I have too much free time. There's so much I could fill the free time with, I can't make decisions. So I do nothing. I am a wild turkey, I am a wild turkey.

MASHA   Really? How alarming. (*softer, to Vanya*) What's the matter with her?

VANYA   She's referring to falling out of bed. She's fine. Masha, you look wonderful as usual. But what did you say about a Snow White costume?

MASHA   Oh did I forget to tell Sonia?

SONIA   Um . . . probably. Tell me what?

MASHA   Well I got a lovely invitation from that extremely wealthy woman who bought the Dorothy Parker house up the road. She's one of our neighbors here, and she's dying to get to know people in the area, and so she's throwing a costume party. And she asked me to come.

VANYA   Well she hasn't asked us to come.

MASHA   Well you're not famous. She's inviting famous people and literary people, and interesting people. And, of course, you and Sonia are very interesting. And I told her that, so she wants both of you to come with me and Spike tonight.

VANYA   Spike?

Enter Spike, carrying a large garment bag, which holds the costume, and a shepherd's crook. He finds somewhere to hang up or put down the garment bag and the crook.

SPIKE (*friendly, charming*)   Yup, that's my name. Don't wear it out.

VANYA I'll try not to.

SPIKE Okay, I got the costume and this weird shepherd's thing.

MASHA Thank you, Spike.

SONIA Is Spike the name you were given at birth?

SPIKE No, it's my acting name. My real name was Vlad. But my agent said that that was hard to hear, and I was wearing my hair all spikey that day, and he said, why don't you call yourself Spike. And so I do.

MASHA Spike is a very gifted actor. He was almost cast in the sequel to *Entourage, Entourage 2*. HBO thought he was wonderful.

SPIKE Yeah, I should've gotten that part.

MASHA But, darling, you came very close. They brought you in to network. You were down to the last three.

SPIKE Yeah. And they put me up in a fancy hotel.

MASHA Well, of course.

SONIA Maybe you'll come close to getting another part soon.

MASHA Well next time he'll *get* the part.

SPIKE Yeah, it's only a matter of time.

VANYA I'm sorry, who is Spike? Is he your driver?

MASHA He's my beloved!

VANYA He looks ten.

MASHA Oh, Vanya darling, don't exaggerate. He's 29 if he's a day. And I'm only 41. Possibly 42.

Masha and Spike kiss with abandon and passion.

SONIA Hello. You're not alone in the room. Hello.

MASHA Sorry, it's all rather new for me.

SONIA Really? You've had five husbands.

SPIKE I like older women.

VANYA I'm relieved to hear it.

SPIKE Hey, a spark is either there or it's not, right, Mashie?

MASHA Isn't he adorable?

VANYA He's attractive. I'm not sure if he's adorable.

SONIA Really. Every time I see you, Masha, you make me feel bad. First you don't notice me in the room somehow, and say hello to me as an afterthought. And now here you are nearing your dotage, and you've hooked up with some young stud. While I am forced to live through a succession of tedious days and tedious nights, and I never have fallen in love with anyone. Nor anyone with me. I'm sorry I was adopted into this family. I wish I had been left in the orphanage, and killed myself. Excuse me.

Sonia exits upstairs.

SPIKE Wow, intense.

MASHA Oh, she's always been jealous of me, I'm really sick of it. I can't help if I'm beautiful and intelligent and talented and successful, can I?

VANYA No, I guess you can't.

SPIKE But the unhappy orphanage lady thinks I'm a stud, that's nice. (*He walks over to Vanya, and says provocatively*) What about you? Do you like how I look?

VANYA What?

MASHA Now, Spike, I'm sure Vanya thinks you're a perfectly nice-looking young man. Let's leave it at that. (*to Vanya*) He craves attention slightly. But all good actors do.

SPIKE I'm hot!

VANYA   Oh yes? Shouldn't you leave that for others to say?

SPIKE   (*laughs good naturedly*)   No, I mean I'm warm. The air is warm, I'm *hot!* (*looking out the window*) That pond that's out there. Can you swim in it?

VANYA   Swim in it? It's not very deep. You can wade in it.

SPIKE   Yeah. Maybe I'll do that.

MASHA   Really, darling, you want to wade in a pond?

SPIKE   Yeah, it's a hot day.

MASHA   I guess it is. There are frogs in the pond, you know.

SPIKE   I like frogs.

MASHA   Did you bring a swimsuit?

SPIKE   No, I can just strip to my underwear. See you later, babe, I'm gonna go cool off in the pond.

MASHA   Well, if that's what you want, darling. (*to Vanya*) He's so unpredictable.

Very comfortable, but also liking people to watch him, Spike takes his shoes off, then takes his shirt off, then takes his pants off. With abandon, he throws his clothes onto a couch or chair. He puts his shoes back on. He is now only in his underwear. He looks very good. He starts toward the pond, but gives Masha a quick kiss on his way out.

SPIKE   See you later!

He moves quickly out of the room, but oddly ruffles Vanya's hair on his way outside. It's a playful gesture but Vanya finds it strange. Spike happily exits onto the grass, looking forward to wading and frogs . . .

MASHA   The younger generation is like that. They strip to their underwear right in front of everybody.

VANYA   Did he do that because he knows I'm gay?

MASHA   I rather think he did that because he knows I'm straight.

VANYA   Well it's very peculiar. Did you tell him I'm gay?

MASHA   No, why would I? And are you gay? I'm sorry, did we have some conversation I forgot?

VANYA   No, I guess we didn't. I just . . . assumed you assumed.

MASHA   Oh, I did. I just thought maybe you were still in denial. Or had become asexual from so many years of abstinence. Oh, I've been a bad sister. I'm sorry, darling. Where is Sonia? Oh that's right, I upset her. Well I'll apologize later.

VANYA   I must say, I'm a trifle surprised to see you with this young, young man. How old is he?

MASHA (*takes his hand*)   Oh, Vanya dear, I'm so happy I'm with Spike. He's so adventurous and free, he gives me energy. We've been together 3 months.

VANYA   Well he's handsome. Is he a good idea?

MASHA   Don't be judgmental. I've been very lonely for several years ever since Robert left me for Heidi Klum.

VANYA   Heidi Klum?

MASHA   I just say that to make myself feel better. He left me for someone who looked a little like Heidi Klum. So I comfort myself with saying it was she. Still I haven't been able to hold on to my husbands, I don't know why. I'm talented, charming, successful—and yet they leave me. They must be insane.

Enter Sonia.

SONIA   Why is that young man naked in the pond?

VANYA   He's naked? (*looks out the window, interested*) Sonia, he's wearing underpants. That's not naked.

SONIA   Well, underpants, naked, it's the same to me.

VANYA   You need glasses.

SONIA I need a life. I need a friend. I need a change. But nothing ever changes.

MASHA Now, now, please don't get down in the dumps.

SONIA That's easy for you to say. You have a life, you have a career.

MASHA Oh, I wish you wouldn't feel jealous of me. It just exhausts me. Even if you were an actress, God forbid, we wouldn't ever go up for the same parts. I'm a leading lady, while you are much more of a . . .

VANYA Masha, I don't think you should finish that sentence.

SONIA Thank you, Vanya.

VANYA You're welcome, Sonia.

MASHA Well, it's not as if my career has been without disappointments, just like your life, Sonia. I've suffered too. I'm a movie star, but am I known as a classical actress on the stage?

SONIA No you're not.

MASHA Exactly! That's a path I didn't get to take. Remember when that famous acting teacher was going to cast me as Masha in *Three Sisters*. He said I was born to play that role. Imagine how wonderful I would've been. (*to Vanya and Sonia, suddenly acting the lines:*) "Oh my sisters, let us go to Moscow! To Moscow, let us go."
    I would have said that with an ache in my voice and my soul, and it would have been heartbreaking. I feel the public doesn't know how heartbreaking I can be. (*genuinely*) Oh missed opportunities! Regret, regret, regret!

SONIA Regret, regret!

MASHA Please don't change the focus to yourself, Sonia. I'm talking now. You can talk later.

SONIA When?

25

MASHA   4:30. (*back to her story*) Oh that famous acting teacher said I was born to play the classics. And that once I did *Three Sisters*, he said I would have one classical triumph after another. I'd be the American Judi Dench. But I had to go do that movie about the nymphomaniac serial killer. It was a terrible script, but I was so good in it that it became this enormous hit and, of course, we made five of them eventually. Did you see all of them?

VANYA   Oh yes, we certainly did. We liked you very much. They were extremely violent, though. Sonia had to look away from the screen a lot.

SONIA   Yes, I did.

MASHA   Oh darling, sensitive, tedious Sonia. You can't face life, can you?

   Sonia begins to respond, but Masha stops her.

No, don't answer. You can talk at 4:30.

SONIA   Why 4:30?

MASHA   That's my nap time. (*when Sonia looks horrified*) I'm kidding, I'm kidding—4:30 is the cocktail hour, a half an hour early. I usually have a Black Russian. And a drink as well. Oh, I'm amusing myself, sorry. (*focuses back on her story*) Anyway, as I was saying that movie, *Sexy Killer*, really changed my life—it took me from being a respected actress to being a global celebrity. And there is a difference. "Fame, thou glittering bauble." Who said that?

VANYA   Captain Hook.

MASHA   The real Captain Hook?

VANYA   There wasn't a real Captain Hook. He was just in *Peter Pan*.

MASHA   "Fame, thou glittering bauble." Such an interesting thing for a pirate to say. And then they begged me to do a sequel, and it seemed inescapable to me. We made 5 of them. And those movies made me millions. But my point was the theater lost a great tragic classical actress when I didn't play my namesake Masha in that famous acting teacher's production of *Three Sisters*. That's my point!

SONIA You keep talking about this famous acting teacher. Who are you referring to?

MASHA Derek Seretsky.

SONIA Who?

MASHA Derek Seretsky. Maybe he wasn't famous. He was famous to me.

VANYA When did you study with him?

MASHA Oh, many years ago, I can't remember dates or decades. I just live. I recall I had three fabulous sessions with him. He taught a combination of Stanislavskian sense memory mixed with Meisner repetition technique.

I'd say "Oh, Olga, let's go to Moscow" and he'd say back to me "Oh, Olga, let's go to Moscow?" And I'd say, "Oh Olga—let's GO to Moscow." And he'd say "Oh, oh, oh, Olga, let's go to MosCOW." And then I said, "Ho, ho, ho, let's go to Moscow, Olga. Moscow, Moscow, Olga. Oh, Oh, Olga, let's go!"

I'm sorry, this is sounding incredibly false as I'm saying it. It makes one think I would've been horrible in *Three Sisters*. Maybe I would have been. (*suddenly shouts emphatically*) No, no, I would've been great! Let's not talk about it anymore. Let's talk about something else. Sonia, what's new with you?

SONIA I'm not allowed to speak until 4:30.

MASHA Everyone's so touchy here. No, you can talk.

SONIA How old is Spike exactly?

MASHA Let's talk about something fun. We're going to a party tonight, and a costume one at that. I love costume parties.

SONIA We don't have any costumes to wear, Masha.

MASHA Yes, you do. I asked Hootie Pie to organize some costumes for both of you, and they're in the car.

VANYA (*worried*)   Hootie Pie?

SONIA (*worried*)   Who is Hootie Pie?

MASHA   Why do you both look frightened?

Enter Cassandra, she's clearly been listening just off-stage.

CASSANDRA   I was right! Didn't I say Beware of Hootie Pie? I saw this coming, I warned you, but did you listen?

MASHA   Who is this person?

CASSANDRA   I wonder, could I get your autograph? My niece is a big fan of yours, she loves all those *Sexy Killer* movies.

MASHA   Oh how nice. I'd be happy to give her an autograph.

CASSANDRA   Make it out to Rebecca Sue, If you would. (*hands Masha a small card to sign*)

MASHA   All right. Becky Sue.

Masha signs the card, gives it back to Cassandra.

MASHA   Give my best to your niece. And who are you?

VANYA   This is Cassandra, she's our cleaning woman.

CASSANDRA   They never listen to me. I warned them about bats, and then there were bats. I warned them about breaking a toe, and a toe was broken. And this morning, I had a sense that Vanya and Sonia must beware of an entity called Hootie Pie.

MASHA   Well, she's not an entity.

VANYA   What is she then?

MASHA   She's my new assistant and completely devoted to me.

SONIA   It might be fun to go to a party, Vanya. I've wanted to see the house Dorothy Parker used to live in. Do you know her suicide poem? It was very witty, at the same time it actually made you want to kill yourself.

28

MASHA You know, I'm feeling rather hungry after my long drive. (*to Cassandra*) Would you mind making a light lunch for all of us?

CASSANDRA I am a cleaning lady. I am not the cook.

MASHA Could you not make us a modest repast? A salad Niçoise. An artichoke quiche perhaps. I would certainly pay you something for your trouble.

CASSANDRA I don't want to.

MASHA All right. Give me back that autograph I gave you.

CASSANDRA No.

MASHA Yes.

CASSANDRA All right, I'll make you lunch. (*exits, grouchy*)

MASHA Don't feed us your anger, please.

SONIA I'm starting to like the idea of a party. A party could be fun. Maybe I'd meet someone. Or in any case, the people there wouldn't know me and wouldn't have a bad impression of me, and maybe I could be witty at the party, and make new friends. What do you think, Vanya?

VANYA (*thinks it doubtful, but tries to agree*) Uh, sure.

MASHA I'm going as Snow White. I wanted Spike to go as Prince Charming, but I think he's going as a rap star. You must talk him into Prince Charming, would you, Vanya? And Hootie Pie came up with good ideas for both of you. Vanya, you can be one of the seven dwarfs, we think you should go as Grumpy.

VANYA I don't want to go as Grumpy.

MASHA It suits you.

VANYA No. If anything I should go as Doc. The one with the wire rim glasses and the beard. I think I look like him now that I'm older.

MASHA Well I suppose you can be Doc. He's not as memorable as Grumpy.

SONIA What costume did you bring for me?

MASHA Hootie and I thought you could go as Dopey.

SONIA What?

MASHA You know, the dwarf Dopey. And he's clean-shaven, so you wouldn't have to wear a beard.

SONIA I don't want to be Dopey! (*starts to cry*)

MASHA Darling, Sonia, forgive me. Which dwarf do you want to be?

SONIA I don't want to be a dwarf!

MASHA But, darling, I only brought two dwarf costumes. That's all Hootie Pie made up for me.

SONIA Fuck Hootie Pie!

MASHA Well, who do you want to be then? Goodness, all this fuss over costumes, it's just a party for heaven's sake.

SONIA I don't want to go as your dwarf. I want to go as . . . Jean Harlow. Or Marlene Dietrich.

MASHA Well I must say. I'm the one who was invited, and I'm going as Snow White. And obviously the rest of you should go in a costume connected to ME. Snow White is the central figure. I can't have you traipsing around, pathetically trying to be Marlene Dietrich.

VANYA Oh dear. This is getting out of control. Masha, Sonia doesn't want to be a dwarf and I must say I understand her feeling. I don't mind going as a dwarf, I'm happy to be a dwarf. But isn't there some other fairy tale figure that's appealing that Sonia could go as?

MASHA No, it has to be from *Snow White*, it has to be connected. Oh I have an idea. Sonia, do you want to go as the wicked witch with the wart on her nose?

Sonia stands up to Masha with firmness.

SONIA I do not wish to be a witch with a wart on my nose, Masha. I am going to go as the BEAUTIFUL evil Queen BEFORE she turns into the wicked witch. The one who says mirror, mirror on the wall, and so on. And I will look good in my costume!

MASHA Well I don't know that Hootie Pie can organize such a costume by tonight . . .

SONIA I will get the costume myself. There's a second-hand store in Upper Black Eddy. I will drive there this afternoon and I will find some sort of Beautiful Evil Queen costume that I will wear tonight.

VANYA Good for you, Sonia.

MASHA Well I don't see why you're both ganging up on me. You can see why I don't come here that much. And what kind of name for a town is Upper Black Eddy? Pennsylvania scares me sometimes.

SONIA Well what kind of name do you prefer? (*contemptuously*) Manhattan? The Upper West Side?

MASHA Sonia, I'm sorry if I offended you about the dwarf costume. But you do whatever makes you happy. I only want to be around happy people.

Sonia looks out the front window, by chance.

SONIA Who is that young woman Spike is talking to down at the pond?

MASHA (*immediately worried*) What young woman?

All three of them look out the window. Masha looks quite concerned and leaves the morning room quickly and stands on the grass, calling out toward the pond.

MASHA Spike! Spike! We need you up here. (*she comes back in to the room*) He can't hear me. Do you have a gong or anything?

VANYA What for?

31

MASHA I just want to make a noise, and summon him back.

SONIA We don't have a gong. You probably could take a big pot and bang it with a metal spoon.

MASHA Oh what a good idea, thank you, Sonia. (*goes off to kitchen*) Cassandra! I need a pot!

Masha exits toward the kitchen.

SONIA (*not confrontational; being honest*) I don't think you believe I'll meet anyone at this party. I think you looked at me with pity as I said that.

VANYA (*trying to be kind*) No, not at all. One should stay open to unexpected possibilities. I think you could meet someone there tonight.

SONIA Our lives are over, aren't they?

VANYA Yes, I think so.

SONIA Still I'll go to the party. And I won't go dressed as a dwarf.

Reenter Masha with a big pot and a big metal serving spoon.

MASHA I had to struggle with her to get a pot out of the kitchen. And she started to do all that "Beware this" and "Beware that" business. She's very difficult.

Masha goes outside again and makes very loud noise banging the pot.

MASHA (*calling*) Spike! Spike! We need you! Spike!

VANYA Oh look, he's seen her. He's waving.

MASHA (*calling*) Lunch is almost ready. (*seeing something*) No, don't bring the girl. There's not enough lunch. Tell her to go home.

VANYA Oh, the girl's coming with him.

Masha comes back into the house, angry.

MASHA I don't know if he can't hear me or is pretending he can't. Oh God. She's very pretty. And she's very young.

SONIA Masha, I'm sure the power of your money and your connections will keep Spike at your side for a long time.

MASHA Oh. That's a comforting point. Thank you. I shouldn't be intimidated by a young girl, should I? Plus I don't actually know how pretty she is, maybe she's hideous.

Enter Spike and NINA. *Nina is in her early 20s, and is very pretty and luminous.*

SPIKE Look who I met at the pond.

MASHA Oh did you meet someone?

SPIKE Yes. She's visiting her aunt and uncle who live next door. And you're her favorite actress, and she came over here hoping to meet you.

MASHA Oh how charming. Welcome, lovely little nymph.

NINA Hello. Oh, it's so thrilling to meet you. My aunt and uncle said to me you mustn't go bother them, and plus she's never ever there, but then we had our binoculars out and we saw your car drive up, and I thought, I can't believe she's here! I can meet Masha Hardwicke. A woman who has achieved fame and success in theater and in motion pictures. I LONG to make theater my life, and you're an idol to me. And I'm only here for three days, and I hoped I could meet you, but then I didn't dare think it would actually happen. But it has.

MASHA (*sort of friendly*) Yes, you're meeting me. Hello. Hello.

NINA And today is my name day, can you imagine? Americans like to say "birthday," but I like to say "name day" because I love the plays of Anton Chekhov and Irina in *Three Sisters* is always saying "it's my name day."

MASHA Ah, well. It's lovely to meet you. You're so very pretty and luminous, and full of youthful hope and enthusiasm. I wonder if it makes it hard for older people to be around you.

NINA I'm sorry, what?

MASHA   Nothing. My unconscious was speaking, pay no mind. Happy name day. What is your name by the way?

NINA   I'm Nina.

MASHA   (*furious*)   GOD DAMN IT!

VANYA   What's the matter?

MASHA   That crazy psychic in the kitchen told me to "Beware of Nina" and now her fucking name is Nina!!!

NINA   What? I'm sorry, what?

SONIA   Hello, Nina, I have a feeling no one is going to introduce me, I'm kind of like furniture in the room rather than a person. But I'm Sonia, Masha's sister. Although I'm adopted and don't really belong here. Or anywhere. And this is my brother Vanya.

VANYA   Hello, Nina. Happy name day.

NINA   How lovely to meet you. And what a funny joke about the furniture.

Everyone looks confused.

SPIKE   I told Nina I'd introduce her to my manager. And I invited her to the costume party.

MASHA   (*taking that in*)   You invited her. How nice. I have an idea! Spike, why don't we skip the party and hop in the car and race back to New York City right this minute. I suddenly want to see a Broadway show. How late is the half-price ticket booth open, does anyone know?

SPIKE   No, I wanna go to the party. And Nina is so excited to meet you. She just worships you. (*a bit flirtatiously*) As do I.

MASHA   (*taking in what he said, a bit mollified*)   Well, that's sweet of you to say, Spike. I . . . uh . . . am flattered Nina looks up to me. Hello, Nina. Happy name day.

NINA   Thank you.

Enter Cassandra.

CASSANDRA Lunch will be a little delayed. I dropped the omelettes on the floor. I'm going to have to start over. (*sees Nina, points at her*) What did I say? BEWARE OF NINA!

MASHA Cassandra, Nina is visiting from next door, and she's a lovely aspiring actress.

CASSANDRA Well, I warned you, but the curse of Apollo keeps everyone from acting on my warnings. (*feels drawn to make a bit of a speech*)

Oh mystery and misery, descends upon me like a thundercloud,
Pregnant with rain and Jupiter's arrows.
The terrible burden of true prophecy, of my unwanted but
    unstoppable prelude.
Look out, look out—all around us are lions and tigers and bears.
Oh my, the omelette is a failure, I crush it beneath my foot.

The libation bearers bring guts and entrails
And parents' children chopped up and served in a shepherd's pie.
Something tastes wrong with it—little wonder!
Next time you won't go killing Agamemnon, will you?
He's already dead. My car needs to be inspected,
How can I keep all these facts in my head when I see calamity and
    colossus
Lumbering up the walkway?
Oh wretches, oh misery, oh magical mystery tour.
Beware the future. I know you will not abide me,
You ignore because I am not tall.
But I am right! I see disaster ahead for all of you!
Lunch in about 20 minutes!

She strides out.

NINA Oh she's a wonderful actress too. What was that from, what she just recited?

MASHA It was from one of the Greek tragedies, I think. But I believe she embellished it slightly.

NINA Tell me . . . I wonder if this is a stupid question. But what is the difference between acting in a movie and acting on stage?

MASHA No, it's not stupid at all. In film, you are acting in front of a camera, and you need to speak in a normal voice. And on stage, you are in a sort of wooden box in front of people who are looking at you and you must speak more loudly. So that they can hear you.

NINA I see, yes. What was your favorite role on stage?

MASHA My favorite role on stage. Well I loved all the Ibsen I did, and the Chekhov, and the Shakespeare. Google me when you go home. Besides I'm not the only actor in the room. Spike is wonderfully talented. He was almost cast in *Entourage 2*.

NINA Yes, he told me.

MASHA Spike, why don't you . . . (*suddenly notices he's still in his underwear*) Goodness, you're still in your underwear. Spike, dear, why don't you do the opposite of a strip tease, and put your clothes back on, and then you can show Nina the audition you did. I coached him.

SPIKE Oh, okay. (*he starts to put his clothes back on*) First I have to take my shoes off, so I can put my pants back on. (*he takes his shoes off*) And now it's time for the jeans. (*he pulls on his jeans, but very seductively; gyrating his body*) But I'm not going to zip the zipper up all the way. Not just yet.

Everyone has been staring at him, not quite sure what else to do. Vanya moves closer and sits on the floor, watching him unabashedly.

MASHA Maybe we don't need to watch Spike while he's dressing.

SPIKE No it's all right, I don't mind.

Masha gets focused on arranging some of the furniture for the upcoming audition. Spike is getting into his reverse striptease.

I'm going to leave the zipper a little undone. Because I know I'm going to tuck in my shirt when I get to putting that on.

SONIA Should we leave the room until he's finished?

SPIKE No, I'm almost done. Now I could do the shirt first, or I could do the belt first. I think I'll do the belt.

He kind of plays with the belt before putting it on. Or he puts it on, but makes a big deal of it . . . Masha refocuses on him as he does more sexual gyrating . . .

MASHA What are you doing? Are you insane?

SPIKE (*he was just obeying*) You told me to do a reverse striptease.

MASHA Did I? Well I'm sure I didn't mean it. Just get dressed, for God's sake.

SPIKE Okay, okay. (*to Nina*) The older generation is all uptight about their bodies.

MASHA Okay, now your clothes are back on, very good, thank you. We all had a lovely time.

SPIKE Gosh, you're in a weird mood today.

NINA Well maybe I should be going.

SPIKE No. I was going to show you my audition. Unless you don't want to see.

NINA No, I'd love to see.

Everyone sits down to watch him.

SPIKE The original series *Entourage* is about this young actor who's making it big in the movies, and it's about the guys who hang around him—his friends, his manager, his agent. Everyone wants a piece of him.

NINA I'd be so nervous if I ever had to audition. But I'd be so thrilled too.

SPIKE Yeah, it's tough to audition. I was real lucky to have a pro like Masha coach me.

MASHA Yes, let's get to the audition now.

SPIKE So I was auditioning for the spin-off series *Entourage 2*. And it has a different setup because in this one there's an up-and-coming actor who's starting to make it big in the movies, but he's played by somebody else, so the implication is it's another character.

MASHA It's not an implication. He is another character.

SPIKE (*kind of laughs, realizes he got confused*)   Right. I know that. His name is Bradley Wood, and he's the lead. And in *this* version, his entourage is this old dame who's his agent, and this young guy on coke who's his manager, and his best friend from high school who's a girl who has a crush on him but she has this disease that gives her convulsions so she can never kiss anybody, cause she gets convulsions. And I live next door to a rabbi who's played by Judd Hirsch. But he's not on every week.

MASHA Yes, yes. Let's move it along, pacing, pacing.

SPIKE Okay, and he's been having an affair with his older agent lady, but he's thinking of moving on to another agent. So the scene is between Bradley Wood and his lady agent.

NINA I see.

SPIKE Okay, he comes into the room, and the manager is there. "Hey, good-looking. How's tricks?" And Masha used to read the other lines. Do you remember them, Masha?

MASHA Kind of. But I think you should try to do it as a monologue . . . we'll all intuit what the other lines are.

SPIKE Oh, okay.

He likes the challenge. He changes his body language, and begins the scene, maybe unbuttons his top three shirt buttons.

Hey, good-looking. How's tricks? (*dutifully ad-libs listening to make it a monologue*) What? Who told you that? Hey, don't cry. Come on, give me a smile. Besides, it's not definite. (*pointedly listens*) Well . . . yeah, it's true, I did meet with some agents at CAA. I thought they were real impressive. I mean, they can call up Sandy Bullock, they can call up Julia Roberts. You gotta face it, you don't know that caliber of person. What? (*he listens*) What about loyalty? What about my career? What about my getting ahead? Yeah, I know you put in a lot of time with me. But I put a lot of time in with you too. And I don't know . . . I think I might like CAA better. What? (*listens*) Oh, that. Well, yeah, just cause I go to another agent doesn't mean we have to stop sleeping together occasionally. Well I think it's occasional. I mean I sleep with other people too. I want to be successful, I can't just sleep with one old broad all the time. Oh, I'm sorry, don't cry. I think of "old broad" as a term of affection. (*listens*) Oh yeah? Well fuck you!

He bows, smiles.

MASHA Wasn't that good?

Masha leads the applause. Nina is sincere and thinks it was good. Vanya and Sonia are a touch shell-shocked but applaud anyway.

NINA Oh that was wonderful. I can sense great things in your future.

SPIKE Yeah, cool. Thanks.

Enter Cassandra.

CASSANDRA Luncheon is served. It's Campbell's soup and tuna fish sandwiches. I was only asked to make lunch for 4, but I did stretch it to 5, though the sandwiches are a little skimpy with the tuna fish. (*exits*)

MASHA Well, the lunch sounds repellent, but shall we go in?

NINA (*to Masha*) Oh you're so kind to invite me to lunch, but I mustn't impose any further. And you did invite me to the costume party, so I'll come back for that, shall I?

MASHA Yes, dear. That would be lovely. Why don't you come over at 7:30, it's just a little ways away, at the Dorothy Parker house.

NINA Wonderful. I'll see you later. It was a pleasure to meet you all. (*to Masha*) And a special honor to meet you, Miss Hardwicke.

Nina exits. Bit of a pause from everyone.

MASHA Well. That was . . . fun. I need to go lie down. I think I'll forgo the tuna fish sandwiches.

SONIA And I need to drive to Upper Black Eddy, and find a costume.

MASHA Spike, do you want to take a nap with me?

SPIKE I think I'll have the soup and sandwich.

MASHA I think I'm getting a headache. Excuse me.

SPIKE I'll come up in a bit and give you a massage.

MASHA That would be lovely, thank you. (*exits to upstairs*)

SONIA Vanya, do you want to come with me?

VANYA You know, the soup and sandwich doesn't sound so bad to me. I think maybe I'll stay and have lunch.

SONIA All right. See you later then. Goodbye, Spike. (*exits*)

SPIKE So it's just you and me, pal.

VANYA Yes.

SPIKE Time to tie on the old feedbag, right? (*friendly, but has a flirtatious vibe; he sort of does with everyone*)

VANYA Oh yes, right.

SPIKE Tell me, did you like my audition? Feel free to be honest.

VANYA Um . . . I liked it very much. I don't see why HBO didn't cast you. I think they must be . . . muddled.

SPIKE Yeah, screwed up, huh? Come on, old guy, let's go chow down, and you can tell me more of what you thought.

They start to exit to the dining room.

VANYA (*not sure what else he can say*) Tell you more? All right . . .

They exit to the dining room.

SCENE 2

Sound of a doorbell.

MASHA (*calling from off-stage*) Come in! The door is open.

Enter Masha dressed like Snow White, and carrying a shepherd's crook. Her costume is based on the old Walt Disney cartoon: she has a bright blue bodice, with puffy sleeves around her shoulders. She has a big yellow skirt to the floor, and a red bow in her hair. She looks good, but it's a somewhat dominating costume. It is possible she is still putting parts of the costume on.

Meanwhile Nina has let herself in, and enters the Morning Room. She is dressed like a princess. She holds a fairy wand.

NINA Hello. Oh my, you look beautiful.

MASHA Oh dear, I didn't talk to you about costumes, did I? Whatever are you dressed as?

NINA I didn't have anything, but my aunt and uncle took me to K-Mart, and I'm a princess.

MASHA Oh you are? I see. I didn't get it. I thought you were a child dressed in her mother's clothes.

NINA I'm sorry. I wasn't expecting to go to a costume party.

MASHA No, that's quite evident.

NINA What are you dressed as?

41

MASHA What am I dressed as? You can't tell?

NINA I think so. Are you that silent screen actress from the old movie who lives in a mansion and says "I'm ready for my close-up, Mr. DeMille"? What's her name?

MASHA No, I'm not Norma Desmond. Although when I'm around you, I feel like her. You must be reading my aura.

NINA I never really saw the movie. I just saw the clip where she says "ready for my close-up." So who are you dressed as?

MASHA I'm dressed as Snow White. The Walt Disney version.

NINA I've never seen *Snow White and the Seven Dwarfs*. Is it like *The Little Mermaid*?

MASHA (*a touch annoyed*) No. One's about a mermaid, and the other's about dwarfs.

NINA I see.

MASHA Now since I'm Snow White, I feel all the other people going to the party with me must *relate* to Snow White.

Enter Vanya dressed like one of the seven dwarfs. Big floppy knit cap, and a pumpkin-colored shirt with a belt around and brown pants.

MASHA You see—like that. That's Grumpy, one of the seven dwarfs.

VANYA Doc.

MASHA Right. Doc. Another one of the seven dwarfs.

VANYA You look lovely, Nina.

MASHA No she doesn't. She looks like a child dressed for Halloween. I'm afraid I can't have it.

NINA (*sad but obedient*) Oh. Well maybe I can't go then. I'm sorry I didn't have the right costume.

VANYA Masha . . .

MASHA No, no, Nina. I'm not saying you can't go to the party. I'm so sorry. I'm really being a bully, but when you're my age—whatever that age is—you get used to having your way. I suppose I'm monstrous, but lovable monstrous, I hope. Besides, the good news is I have an extra costume that DOES relate to Snow White, and if you'll just put it on, then we'll all be very happy. Now wait here, I have to ask Spike where he put it.

NINA Oh I can't wait to see what he's wearing.

MASHA Really? Why?

NINA Well, I can't wait to see what everyone's wearing.

MASHA Okay.

VANYA What is he going as?

MASHA He's going as Prince Charming. It took a long time to convince him, so everyone tell him he looks sexy. Not you, Nina. Vanya, you tell him. I'll be right back. (*Masha suddenly takes both of Nina's hands*) Thank you, Nina, for being so cooperative. (*ends the moment, moves on, exits to the second floor*)

NINA I wonder what costume she has for me.

VANYA I'm afraid I know. I believe you're going to be a dwarf like me. Dopey.

NINA I'm just so happy to be included. I love to be around artistic people, who create things, who act, who value the arts.

VANYA Well Masha obviously fits that. I'm afraid Sonia and I are just . . . two lumps on a log.

NINA Oh I don't think so. I feel you both have hidden reservoirs that just haven't been tapped. Or maybe you're secretly creating things, and not telling anyone.

VANYA That's remarkable that you say that. I have been writing something . . . I haven't told anyone, not even Sonia.

NINA I thought so. I sensed it. Is it a TV pilot?

VANYA No, it's a play. In progress. And I was thinking of that play Konstantin writes in *The Seagull*. And it's very experimental and mysterious, and I can never tell if it's meant to be a play ahead of its time or just a play that's . . . rotten. And so I thought I might like to write my own version of that play, but relate it to now and see if it would . . . be good or not.

NINA Oh I'm so honored you told me this. I feel certain it's good. I always feel so sorry for Konstantin when I read that play, they were so mean to him.

VANYA Well, life is hard for everyone, I guess.

NINA You remind me of my uncle, only nicer and more artistic. He burps a lot and doesn't speak much. But you don't burp that I've noticed, and you're quiet but then you speak when spoken to. May I call you Uncle Vanya?

VANYA If you like.

NINA Why don't I do a reading of your play tomorrow for everyone?

VANYA Oh I don't know if I want the others to hear it. It may be terrible. I wrote something when I was little, and my father joked and said it was pathetic.

NINA How is that a joke?

VANYA Good question.

NINA Let me read it tomorrow. Either privately for you. Or, the braver choice, for everyone.

VANYA All right. I didn't expect to befriend you.

NINA I'm glad you did.

VANYA I thought you were going to be more Spike's friend.

NINA He is awfully handsome.

VANYA Yes, I imagine he is.

NINA Isn't it terrible that attractive people are so charismatic?

VANYA Yes, terrible.

Enter Masha with a box, followed by Spike. Spike is dressed as a romantic fairy-tale prince. Tights, a crown, a loose white shirt with a V-neck which laces up.

MASHA We finally found it.

SPIKE You said she didn't have a costume. She's wearing a costume.

MASHA It doesn't go with Snow White. Nina understands.

SPIKE I think she looks pretty.

MASHA It doesn't matter if she looks pretty if it doesn't relate to Snow White. We all agreed Snow White was the theme.

SPIKE None of us agreed to it.

MASHA Shut up.

NINA It's all right, I want to make Miss Hardwicke happy. I'm willing to wear whatever costume she wants me to.

MASHA Thank you, dear. (*to Spike*) Go get the paper bag for her head, would you? (*to Nina*) No! I'm just kidding. Please call me Masha.

NINA Thank you.

MASHA Now why don't you go change in the bathroom off the kitchen.

SPIKE That's the size of a closet.

MASHA She's a small girl, I'm sure she'll fit fine.

NINA All right, I'll be back soon. (*she exits to the kitchen*)

MASHA Vanya, how do you think Spike looks as a prince?

VANYA I think he looks very good.

MASHA What else.

VANYA He looks sexy. Though for the full effect, maybe he should go in his underwear.

SPIKE That's what I said.

MASHA You have been in your underwear entirely too much today. Let's not argue. I'm turning into a harpy. Let me change my aura. Everyone be quiet a moment.

With her hands she pushes the air around as if that is the upset aura she wants to be rid of. Pushing the aura away makes her feel better. She relaxes her body and breathes easier.

Oh I feel better. Life is good. And Spike, you look wonderful as Prince Charming.

SPIKE Thank you. You make a hot Snow White.

Spike and Masha kiss. Vanya looks away politely.

Enter Sonia. She is in a sparkling sequin gown that takes over the room. She's wearing glittering earrings, bracelets and a tiara. She looks very good. It might be a beautiful, strong turquoise color. She doesn't look like the Evil Queen in Snow White. *But she does look good.*

SONIA (*in a Maggie Smith voice*) Mirror, mirror on the wall. Who is the fairest of them all? Is it me, Sidney? Tonight, let it be me.

MASHA What is that you're doing?

SONIA (*her regular voice*) I'm the Evil Queen from *Snow White*, as played by Maggie Smith on the way to the Oscars.

MASHA Well, Maggie Smith has nothing to do with . . . oh, never mind, I give up, it's fine. You're the Evil Queen, that's what I'll tell everyone.

SONIA (*in Maggie Smith voice*) As played by Maggie Smith about to win an Oscar. Oh, Sidney, do you think I'll win? I already have one

46

Oscar for *Miss Jean Brodie*—(*does her Maggie Smith voice with Scotland accent*) "Little gels, I am in the business of putting old heads on young shoulders"—(*back to the core Maggie Smith voice*)—but it would be lovely to win a second Oscar, my first one is so lonely on the mantelpiece. Do you agree, Sidney? Will I win tonight? Tonight let it be me, Sidney.

SPIKE Sidney? Sidney Kowalski?

MASHA It's Stanley Kowalski, not Sidney Kowalski.

SONIA (*in Maggie Smith voice*) Sidney, I may have to get a little drunk before they read the nominations. Don't go traipsing off to other tables, leaving me unattended. Not tonight, Sidney.

MASHA I don't understand what she's doing.

VANYA Sonia is doing Maggie Smith in *California Suite*. She plays an actress married to a gay man named Sidney, played by Michael Caine, and in the movie they go to the Oscars together.

SONIA (*in Maggie Smith voice*) That's right. In the film she plays an actress nominated for an Oscar who then doesn't win the Oscar, poor thing . . . But in her real life she was nominated for playing the nominated actress, and then went on to WIN it. The nominated actress who lost the Oscar became the nominated actress who won the Oscar. It was all rather Pirandellian. And rather cheeky.

MASHA You look very good tonight, Sonia. (*pause*) I think we should switch costumes.

SONIA What?

MASHA No, I'm kidding. I'm making a self-aware joke about how competitive I am. Spike, go to the kitchen and see if Nina has gotten tangled up in a doorknob or something.

SPIKE Okay.

He exits.

MASHA I don't know why I thought going to a costume party would be fun. And every time I come to this house, I get unhappy.

VANYA Speaking of the house, the storms have been getting much worse, Cassandra says it's climate change and we're all going to be dead in 10 years, but in any case, we need to get the roof repaired.

MASHA Oh, I've been meaning to tell you. I've decided to sell the house. I mean, I pour buckets of money into it, and I'm never here, and neither of you have money to put into the house, and Hootie Pie nicely offered to look at my expenses, and she pointed out I'm pouring all this money into this old house I hardly ever go to.

SONIA I can't believe my ears. We grew up here. Our roots are here.

MASHA Well, let's not be sentimental. I still make movies, but they don't pay me as much as they used to.

VANYA Sonia, "Beware of Hootie Pie" wasn't about the costumes, it was about selling the house.

SONIA Masha, this Hootie Pie is clouding your judgment. Don't throw away the house we love, and we've lived in all our lives. And what about the cherry orchard?

MASHA What cherry orchard?

SONIA We have a large cluster of cherry trees, don't you remember them from childhood?

MASHA Oh slightly, I guess. Aren't there only 9 or 10 of them?

SONIA THEY ARE AN ORCHARD!

MASHA Lower your voice. They're only trees.

VANYA Masha—so you're going to sell the house and put us out on the street??

MASHA Oh nonsense, you can get an apartment.

SONIA But this is our home.

MASHA Goodness, such fuss. I shouldn't have mentioned it now. Forget about it, let's just go enjoy the costume party, all right? Spike! Hurry up! (*to Vanya and Sonia*) Do you wish to ride with us?

VANYA I think Sonia and I will take our own car.

MASHA Yes, that sounds fine. Look, stop looking so upset. Financially I have to be practical. Now let's forget it for now, and go have a lovely time at this party, all right? (*calls out*) Spike, hurry up! I'm going to the car.

Masha exits. Vanya and Sonia look at one another.

Spike and Nina enter from the kitchen. Nina is dressed as Dopey. The costume is way too big for her, though she looks kind of adorable.

SPIKE What was Masha yelling about?

VANYA She's waiting for you in the car.

SPIKE Oh, okay. (*calling in direction of Masha*) Coming!

Spike heads out to the driveway. Nina starts to follow him but crosses back to Vanya and Sonia.

NINA I feel so fortunate. You're all so nice to me here. But can I ask something? How do you think I look?

VANYA I think you look wonderful.

NINA Really? Thank you. And Sonia, you look stunning. Your costume is much better than the Snow White one.

SONIA Yes, I think I have one-upped her tonight. She has ways to win in the long run however.

NINA Oh I sense sadness. Don't be sad. Life is wonderful, isn't it? Oh Uncle Vanya, dear Sonia—this morning I woke up with no hopes for my artistic endeavors, and by this evening I have the chance of an agent through Spike, and I'm going to a party with a world-class actress and movie star. Oh, life is like a long, long pathway in the forest, filled with wonderful surprises ahead. Artistic fulfillment, fame, fortune . . . love. Do you agree?

SONIA (*tough and not agreeing*)   Sure.

VANYA (*kinder*)   Yes, yes. All those things.

Masha calls from outside, or enters an outer room and shouts inside.

MASHA   Hey, Dopey! Get in the car, I don't like waiting for people. People wait for me, not the other way around, okay?

NINA (*to Vanya and Sonia*)   See you at the party.

Masha goes back toward the car, with Nina following close behind. Vanya and Sonia look at each other.

SONIA   Masha is selling the house. And she says "Let's go enjoy the party."

VANYA   I know. We gave up all those years taking care of our parents, but we forgot to make a life for ourselves.

SONIA   Oh God.

VANYA   Do you want to skip going to the party? We could see if there's a cake in the kitchen, and eat the entire thing, and then roll about on the floor until we pass out in a sugar-induced semi-coma.

SONIA   Ah, you're remembering how we spent last New Year's Eve here. That was fun. But I don't want to do that tonight. No, we're dressed in costumes, we never leave the house, I say . . . (*in Maggie Smith voice*) Let's go to the party, Sidney.

Vanya offers his arm; he and Sonia exit.

ACT II

After the party. Sounds of a car driving up. Maybe sounds of voices, not decipherable, out in the driveway.

Sonia and Vanya come in and go to the Morning Room.

VANYA What's the matter with Masha?

SONIA (*in a good mood, enjoying that Masha isn't in a good mood*) I don't think she had a good time.

VANYA She was talking to lots of people. I assumed she was enjoying herself.

SONIA Sssssssh. Here she comes.

Masha comes in, in a bad mood.

MASHA Oh for God's sake. (*calls out to the car*) I don't see why she can't *walk* home. Doesn't she just live next door?

Spike, also annoyed, follows her in.

SPIKE It's dark out. She could fall in a ditch.

MASHA She's young, it wouldn't hurt her.

SPIKE Masha, stop calling out the door that it's all right if Nina falls in a ditch.

MASHA I didn't wish it on her. I just thought . . . well, if you were going to drive her to her door, why didn't you drop her off first, when you and I were in the car . . . and now . . . you're going out on a second trip.

SPIKE Masha, I just drove back here first, not thinking. What are you afraid of? Do you want to drive *with* me, as I drive Nina to her door?

MASHA No. Certainly not. And I'm not afraid of anything. Just don't be long.

SPIKE All right. I'll see you in a bit.

MASHA All right, darling.

SPIKE (*thrown away, bit hard to hear:*) Don't wait up. (*exits*)

MASHA (*to Vanya and Sonia*) I just don't see why he didn't drop her off first. You know what I mean?

VANYA None of us thought of it. I mean she left from here, so it seemed logical to bring her back here.

MASHA Wait a minute. Did he just say "don't wait up"?

VANYA Did he? I'm not sure.

SONIA Yes, he did say that. I was surprised you didn't fall to the ground and hold on to his foot.

MASHA What?

SONIA When he said "don't wait up." I thought you would say something.

MASHA No, he must have said something that sounded like that. I mean he's just taking her next door. It couldn't take longer than 5 minutes.

SONIA Maybe he'll go in and meet her family. Maybe she'll offer him a cup of tea. Or a brandy. And it can take a very long time to sip a brandy. And they'll have a long, long conversation.

MASHA What is the matter with you today? You're so hostile to me.

VANYA Don't fight, you two.

MASHA I just feel nervous about if he said "Don't wait up" or not.

VANYA Maybe he didn't say it. I don't know what he said.

MASHA Everything seems wrong today. And I'm going to give Hootie Pie a piece of my mind. The Snow White costume was a big bust. Nobody knows the Walt Disney version anymore, so they had no idea who I was supposed to be. And Nina, that nasty, grasping young girl, asked me if I was Norma Desmond. And someone else said Little Bo Peep. And several people thought I was a Hummel figurine.

SONIA People seemed to like my costume.

MASHA Well, Sonia, don't be so happy about it. You're happy at my expense.

SONIA Am I? Am I allowed to be happy ONLY when you're happy? Is that one of the rules of being around Masha?

VANYA Let's unwind and not argue. I'm going to go make tea for all of us. Stop talking about upsetting things. Think calming thoughts.

SONIA Can it be Sleepy Time tea?

VANYA Yes, it can.

Vanya exits. Masha and Sonia sit down. They're quiet for a bit.

SONIA I love Sleepy Time tea.

MASHA I prefer caffeinated tea.

SONIA I'm sorry what I said about Spike taking Nina home. Actually, he mumbled, I'm not sure what he said. And I hope he'll be back very soon. I don't want you to be unhappy.

MASHA Thank you.

A moment of peace.

SONIA Though you don't care whether *I'm* unhappy since you want to sell the house out from under us.

MASHA I PAY ALL THE BILLS AND IT'S TOO EXPENSIVE!

SONIA Fine! Vanya and I will get prescription sleeping pills and kill ourselves. Will that make you happy?

MASHA You enjoy complaining too much to kill yourself. You'll go to your grave complaining. And you cheated on your costume tonight. You said you were going as the Evil Queen but no one got "Mirror Mirror" from you, they got Dame Maggie Smith winning a fucking Oscar. If you had gone as a dwarf, my costume would have worked. Snow White needs at least three dwarfs for the costume to make sense.

SONIA Oh stop talking about your costume, I'm sick of hearing about it.

MASHA I should have called up Equity and hired seven Equity actors to be all seven dwarfs, and then you and Vanya could've just stayed home.

SONIA I'm glad we went to the party. And people liked me. (*does Maggie Smith voice*) Yes they did. I had a good time. Didn't I, Sidney?

MASHA I should've known better than to let you choose your own costume. Anyone who wears a tiara and sequins is always going to be the winner.

SONIA Masha, you have won in so many ways throughout your entire life, can you REALLY not survive one night where I wore a costume that people liked more than the one you wore? Not even for *one night* are you willing for me to outshine you?

MASHA You often outshine me.

SONIA When?

MASHA I don't know. When I'm not here, you outshine me. Besides, it's unimportant who preferred whose costume at some stupid party. I'm just having a hard time. Do you mind? I'm getting older, my five marriages didn't work out, I had this young man, I thought, but he seems to be lusting after Nina, and at least five other women at the party. He's clearly oversexed. And I just feel old and vulnerable. Forgive me for having feelings.

SONIA Well I have feelings too! I'm unhappy too! I haven't lived. You've had five marriages, they failed, but you had them. My relationships with men have been limited to "here's your change, ma'am," at the supermarket. I took care of YOUR parents, Vanya and I did, and then we never left because . . . we didn't know how to leave. We became numb during those 15 years taking care of them.

MASHA Well I'm sorry you felt numb, but I was working so I could pay the bills.

SONIA And then when they both got Alzheimer's! His was worse, he was always taking off his clothes, and going to the neighbors' garage where he'd sit naked in their car until they came out to use it. We were always apologizing for him.

MASHA This is all in the past. Get over it.

SONIA You just left us here. If I tried to reach you, you were always filming in Morocco or something. After a while they stopped recognizing me. But they talked about you constantly. "Where is Masha?" they'd say to me. "She's making a fucking movie," I said. And they'd say, "Isn't that wonderful. She's so pretty and delightful." And then I'd change their diapers, all the while thinking why isn't Masha here?

MASHA I was paying the bills! I was paying *your* bills. I paid for the house, the doctors, the food. I paid for the snow plowing. I paid for the lawn care. I paid for the heat, the electricity, I sent you both a monthly stipend because I knew you couldn't work and what you were doing was hard. And I'm sorry if you hated taking care of them, but someone had to earn the money to pay for it all, and it was ME!

SONIA I didn't hate taking care of them. I just said it was hard. And sometimes I liked it. They needed me, they needed Vanya. When they died, I felt sad . . . sadder than you. You didn't cry once at the funerals.

55

MASHA I hide my feelings.

SONIA Nonsense, you parade your feelings. You put them on display on stage and in the movies. It's exhausting to be around you.

MASHA And you exhaust me. Your self-pity exhausts me!

SONIA And I'm glad my costume stole your thunder, and that people liked me as Maggie Smith, and thought I was fun, I liked that. But so what? My life is pointless. I haven't lived! I haven't lived! (*she cries*)

MASHA (*while Sonia is crying*) Well I *have* lived and made my money and messed up all my relationships, and now I have nothing! No one loves me, I have no future, my life is over! (*she cries*)

They both cry violently.

Vanya returns, carrying a tray with a teapot and three cups and saucers. He's shocked by their upset.

VANYA Good God. What's going on here?

SONIA I haven't lived!

MASHA My life is over!

VANYA Oh for God's sake. Cheer up.

Sonia and Masha go back to weeping. Their crying is getting a little less intense, though. Like two hysterical children, they start to get tired and their crying subsides.

VANYA Now, now. Whatever is the matter?

SONIA My life is empty. And I forget something every day. I can't remember the Italian for window or ceiling.

VANYA Window is *finestra,* ceiling is *soffitto.*

SONIA That doesn't sound familiar. I don't think I know Italian.

VANYA Well, you haven't forgotten it then, have you?

SONIA No.

MASHA You're giving her all the sympathy. Give me some.

VANYA All right. I'm sorry you're upset.

MASHA I can't remember things either. I can't remember why I should keep living.

VANYA Now, now, you're just feeling blue.

SONIA Our lives are over. Vanya's too.

MASHA It's true. Let's cry some more.

Masha and Sonia try to cry some more, but their crying lasts only a little while. They're like spent children. Everyone gets quiet for a moment.

VANYA Oh, listen to that silence.

MASHA It's lovely. "True silence is the rest of the mind; it is to the spirit what sleep is to the body, nourishment and refreshment."

VANYA Who said that?

MASHA I don't know. Maybe it's from a play I was in.

VANYA "True silence is the rest of the mind."

Silence. Suddenly sound of the car pulling up.

MASHA (*suddenly wired, back in her drama*)   Is that the car? Does it mean he's come back?

Enter Spike.

SPIKE Oh you're all up. Hi.

MASHA Spike, darling!

Masha embraces Spike enthusiastically, rather over-the-top in her relief.

MASHA Oh, I'm so glad to see you! I was afraid you'd be longer! (*kisses him desperately, but then pulls back, trying to cover her tracks*) Now, I'm not needy. I'm just glad to see you.

SPIKE Well, it's nice to be wanted.

MASHA Oh, you are, darling. Come, let's go to bed. I'm exhausted. I want to forget that horrible party and this stressful day, and sleep in . . . ecstasy.

SPIKE Ecstasy. (*to Vanya and Sonia, rolls his eyes; then back to Masha:*) Well, I'll try . . .

Masha starts to take Spike upstairs, but stops to say good night to Vanya and Sonia.

MASHA Good night, you two. Don't forget: true silence is . . . food for the brain. Oh I forgot already. Never mind.

Masha and Spike exit.

SONIA I'm so exhausted.

VANYA Have some tea.

She sips her tea. So does he.

You were so outgoing at the party tonight, you spoke to many people.

SONIA Many people spoke to me. I enjoyed myself.

VANYA I was amazed to see you so animated. And friendly.

SONIA I think we can thank Maggie Smith for that. And the dress. Masha is right, I think sequins are a girl's best friend.

VANYA Well, you made quite a hit.

SONIA I guess I did. But it wasn't really me. It was because I pretended to be someone else.

VANYA Or the more sanguine interpretation is that you found a different part of your personality and you released it tonight.

SONIA Oh don't be the household Pollyanna. My life is horrible, and don't you forget it. One nice evening in 30 years doesn't count for much.

VANYA All right, fine.

SONIA (*sips her tea*)   Oh, now the tea's lukewarm.

VANYA   Do you want to throw it on the ground?

SONIA   No, I'm too tired.

VANYA   That's good.

They both put their tea down on the table.

VANYA   Oh God, what are we going to do about the house?

SONIA   I am a wild turkey. I have not lived. I am a wild turkey.

VANYA   Me too.

They stare ahead, not too happy. Music, lights dim.

Scene 2

Lights up. Morning. Cassandra comes into the house, looks around quickly to see that no one is downstairs yet.

She is holding some odd Mardi Gras-like stick with colored streamers on it, and is going around the room, shaking it. We can assume she's doing some magical or superstition-related, a "cleansing" ceremony.

Then she picks up a little Snow White doll—the doll is dressed pretty much the same as Masha was dressed last night.

Cassandra takes out a pin, and sticks the doll.

MASHA (*from upstairs, screams*)   Aaaaaaaaaaagghhhh!

Cassandra is surprised and encouraged that the pin sticking worked so quickly. Encouraged, she sticks the pin in the doll again.

MASHA (*from upstairs*)   Aaaaaaaaaaaaaaggghhhh!

Cassandra looks at the doll and gets close to its face. She moves the doll up to her forehead. She is visibly sending her thought waves to Masha through the doll.

59

CASSANDRA Did your brain hear that, you sexy killer, you? (*sends in some additional thoughts*) "I do not want to sell the house, I do not want to sell the house. And whenever I *do* think of selling the house, I get a little pain." (*sticks a pin in the doll again*)

MASHA (*off-stage*) Aaaaaaaaaggghhhhh! Vanya! Vanya, come here.

CASSANDRA Oh, it's bad to use voodoo, but it's for a good cause. (*imparts this thought to the doll:*) Beware of selling the house. You have more money than you need, you greedy movie star. Don't toss your brother and your sister into the trash pile. (*said with a rhythm*) It's a bad chile that puts its loved ones on the trash pile. It's a bad chile that puts its loved ones on the trash pile.

VANYA (*off-stage*) Masha, what's the matter?

MASHA (*off-stage*) There's something wrong with the bed. Or the sheets. There are pins in them.

CASSANDRA Ooooh, I'm thinking of selling the house. (*sticks pin in doll*)

MASHA (*off-stage*) Aaaaaaaaggghh.

VANYA (*off-stage*) But you're not even near the bed.

MASHA (*off-stage*) I'm not making it up.

VANYA (*off-stage*) Wait, I need coffee, do you both want some?

SPIKE (*off-stage*) Yeah, man, that'd be good.

MASHA I can't figure out what this is.

VANYA (*off-stage*) I'll be right back.

Cassandra realizes Vanya is about to come downstairs; she looks at the doll and tries to hide it. Vanya enters and she quickly puts the doll behind her.

VANYA Cassandra!

CASSANDRA Beware!

VANYA Of what?

CASSANDRA Everything.

VANYA Why are you here? This isn't one of your cleaning days.

CASSANDRA I'm worried about you and Sonia. I had presentiments last night. Masha must not sell the house. The market is still soft anyway, doesn't she know that? But it's a bad thing for her to do, she needs to watch over you and Sonia. I'm tired of foretelling the future, but then the bad things happen anyway. I want to *change* the future, I want to *change* this situation.

VANYA Well, goodness, that's very generous of you, Cassandra. I appreciate your concern.

CASSANDRA You're welcome. Why don't I go make that coffee for you?

VANYA That would be nice, thanks.

The conversation has relaxed Cassandra and she forgets about the doll behind her back and lets her arms hang at her side as she starts to go to the kitchen.

VANYA Wait a minute, what's that in your hand?

CASSANDRA Nothing.

VANYA What is that doll you're holding?

CASSANDRA It came in a cereal box.

VANYA Cassandra, is that a voodoo doll?

CASSANDRA Good God, is that what this is?

VANYA That's the exact costume that Masha wore last night. How did you know that?

CASSANDRA I'm psychic. Also, I saw Spike hang it up in the bedroom yesterday.

VANYA And is that why Masha has been screaming this morning?

CASSANDRA I really couldn't say.

VANYA I don't approve of voodoo. Though I admit I'm sort of impressed. You stick the pin in the doll and Masha feels it?

CASSANDRA It's just a pin prick, but it makes its point.

VANYA Well don't do it anymore.

CASSANDRA All right, I won't. You wanna try?

VANYA No.

CASSANDRA You sure?

VANYA No I don't want to try.

CASSANDRA Go ahead, try.

VANYA Well . . . It doesn't hurt much, right?

CASSANDRA That's right. I send her thought waves about the house, then I zap her. I'll tell you when. "I want to sell the house."

Cassandra points, and Vanya sticks a pin in the doll. No noise upstairs.

VANYA Oh, it didn't work.

CASSANDRA That's odd. Well, it just proves my other-worldly powers. Here, let me do it. Masha, listen to my brain: "I want to sell the house." (*sticks pin in the doll*)

MASHA (*off-stage*) Aaaaaaaaaagghhhh!

Vanya is amazed, and Cassandra is pleased. They look excited and happy, maybe laugh even. Or do a happy celebration dance.

Right at this moment, Spike comes in wearing a T-shirt and underpants, and wearing untied sneakers. He's amused that they seem so happy.

SPIKE What are you two so happy about?

VANYA Nothing.

Cassandra realizes she's holding the doll, quickly puts it behind her back.

SPIKE What's behind your back?

CASSANDRA (*pretending to see something behind him*) Oh my God! A bat! Look out!

Cassandra dramatically points behind him. Spike turns around. The second he does Cassandra throws the doll to Vanya, who hides it behind his back. Spike turns back, a bit confused at their motion. Vanya suddenly waves the Mardi Gras streamer stick up and down in front of Spike's face, and surreptitiously throws the doll to Cassandra, who quickly puts it in her bag. Spike is slightly confused but still amused at their seeming playfulness.

SPIKE What bat?

CASSANDRA It must have flown upstairs.

SPIKE I hope Masha doesn't see it. She's already hysterical about whatever these weird pinprick things are.

CASSANDRA Oh, she's having trouble with pricks? Women often do.

SPIKE Ha ha. (*to Vanya*) Is the coffee ready?

VANYA No, I was talking.

Enter Masha in a somewhat elaborate dressing gown, like a movie star of an earlier era. She looks stressed and disheveled, though.

MASHA Is the coffee not ready? I need to call Hootie Pie this morning, and I really need my coffee first. And Spike, darling, you forgot your running shorts. You can't go running in the neighborhood in your underwear. (*hands him the shiny running shorts she's carrying*)

SPIKE Oh, right.

CASSANDRA I'll make the coffee, but before I do, I have a morning warning to impart. (*said with conviction and dramatic intoning:*)

O Citizens of Athens,
the temple of Athena

rocks with ages of wines long past their vintage.
Our vines have tender grapes,
Do not stamp on these grapes.
Or on the hearts of your flesh and blood

Beware the nocturnal flying creatures
Beware the hawk, the eagle, the vulture.
Beware the Hootie Owls of Bucks County.
Avoid all real estate transactions for the next 20 years.
You will sell at a loss!
Wait til the market improves, you foolish citizen of Athens!

And ponder on proximity, how close one thing is to another.
Young men are meant for young women.
Or at least women whose decades are within hailing distance.
You can't hail a taxi that is 30 miles away
So why then hail a young man who is but ten and twenty, while you
are ten and twenty and twenty and a whole bunch of change.

Masha looks furious at Cassandra.

These words come not from me but from the Goddess Athena,
And from the Furies who are furious.
Beware, one of you in this room, I'm not quite sure who.
But the initial is M.
I will go make coffee. (*exits*)

MASHA God, I just can't stand her. (*feels pinprick*) Aaaaaaaaaagggh!
What is that??? These pinprick things. Are they in the air?

VANYA I don't know what it is.

*Enter Sonia in her nightgown. So Vanya is in his nightshirt, Masha is in
her elaborate dressing gown, Spike is in his underpants and T-shirt, and
now Sonia too is in her "sleep" clothes.*

SONIA What was all this screaming going on this morning? Masha,
was that you? And why is Cassandra here?

VANYA She had an impulse to come here today. I'll explain later.

SONIA Is there coffee?

MASHA It's in process. *(sits)* You know I met a real estate person at the party last night, her name is Agnes, and she's from a real estate company called Country Meadows Real Estate. She's going to be calling me sometime this morning.

SONIA Really? Why?

MASHA Why do you think?

VANYA Let's not talk about this right now. Let's at least wait until coffee. Or Armageddon, whichever comes first.

MASHA All right.

SONIA All right.

SPIKE You know, I think I'm going to go for my run.

He pulls on the shiny running shorts Masha brought down.

MASHA Isn't he handsome?

SPIKE I don't think I want the T-shirt. Feel freer without it. *(takes off his T-shirt, hands it to Vanya, makes eye contact)* Here, hold this for me, would you? See you later.

He goes out the front door for his run. Vanya is confused/bothered/ titillated by being given the T-shirt.

VANYA Why does he take his clothes off so much?

SONIA Because he can?

MASHA He's been a little off on this visit. I don't understand all this removal of clothing. I mean in the entertainment industry you do have to be seductive a lot, but I start to think Spike is . . . joking with you a bit, Vanya.

VANYA What do you mean joking?

MASHA Well an actor knows to give the audience what it wants. And really, Vanya, you seem very interested whenever he takes his clothes off.

VANYA Well he keeps doing it in front of us. I don't know where else to look.

MASHA You can read a book.

VANYA All right, the next time he takes his clothes off, I'll read a book. (*hands her the T-shirt*) Here, you hold this, would you, I don't want it.

MASHA I must say he was wonderful in bed last night. (*feels the pinprick suddenly*) Aaaaaaaaaaaghhhhh! What is that???

Enter Cassandra.

CASSANDRA We're out of coffee. I could make you beef bouillon.

MASHA Oh for God's sake, I'm getting a terrible headache. Can someone go to a store and get me some coffee?

SONIA The nearest store is 6 miles. The WaWa.

MASHA The Wa Wa? Like Helen Keller?

SONIA Yes, exactly. Helen Keller learns the word for water, and then they all have coffee.

MASHA Oh God, no coffee. I can't cope.

CASSANDRA I will drive to WaWa and bring you all back coffee. And maybe some donuts?

SONIA Oh donuts, donuts!

CASSANDRA Now the three of you go back to bed for a while, or you're going to be cranky all day. (*exits to the driveway*)

MASHA Yes, I want to go back to bed. Oh, but there are all those pin things still.

VANYA No, I have a feeling it'll be all right for a while.

MASHA Why do you say that?

VANYA Um . . . I don't know. Just an intuition.

SONIA You could sleep in the empty small bedroom on the third floor.

MASHA Oh that's a good idea. Thank you, Sonia. (*exits back upstairs to the bedrooms*)

Sonia looks to the window.

SONIA Oh, the blue heron isn't at the pond. Why do I feel that's a bad omen?

VANYA It's just eating fish and frogs somewhere else. Maybe it'll show up later.

SONIA I hope so.

Sonia and Vanya stare out the window. Sonia in particular looks worried. Music, lights dim to black.

SCENE 3

Music and lights indicate a brief amount of time passing. The morning room is empty.

Enter Nina.

NINA Uncle Vanya? Uncle Vanya? (*Looks around. Looks in the direction of the off-stage stairs.*) Uncle Vanya? I'm here.

Enter Spike from his run. He comes in, and puts his hands on his upper legs and leans over, a kind of post-run stretch. Stands up, sees Nina.

SPIKE Oh, it's Nina. How's it hangin'?

NINA Oh hello. I'm looking for Vanya. I was going to read the play he's written.

SPIKE Oh, he's written a play? Is there a part for a handsome young man?

NINA I haven't read it yet. My, you are in very good condition. I congratulate you.

SPIKE Oh, thanks. Yeah, I figure if you got it, flaunt it.

NINA Oh. I'm still working on projection and interpretation. I guess flaunting will come later.

SPIKE Yeah, 'cause you never know when your big break will happen. Look at *Jersey Shore.*

NINA Oh I don't want to. I like Ingmar Bergman and the Merchant Ivory films. I just saw *Smiles of a Summer Night*, it's beautiful. Have you ever seen it?

SPIKE I don't think so. Who's in it?

NINA Gunnar Bjornstrand, Eva Dahlbeck, and Ulla Jacobsson.

SPIKE Ah. I'll have to miss it sometime.

Enter Vanya.

VANYA Nina, I thought I heard you down here.

SPIKE Where's my T-shirt?

VANYA Masha took it upstairs. She's in the third-floor bedroom.

SPIKE Oh, I'll go see her.

VANYA She said she was getting a very strong headache . . .

SPIKE Okay, I won't expect her to put out. Catch you later.

Spike goes upstairs.

NINA He's so attractive. (*they both look after him*) Except for his personality, of course.

VANYA Yes. I would agree with that. Of course he's young.

NINA Did you bring your play?

VANYA It's a partial play, of course. And it's about the weather. I'm very concerned about it. We've been here 45 years, and the last 6 or 7 years, the weather has been much more violent, and extreme.

NINA Oh yes. Global warming. My uncle doesn't believe in it.

VANYA Well I hope he lives a long, long time and suffers through it. I'm sorry that's not nice to say.

NINA That's all right. So tell me about the play. What's my character like?

VANYA Well, it's not a traditional character, it's a . . . molecule.

NINA It's not a person?

VANYA It has thoughts and feelings, but it's not a person.

NINA Gosh, I wonder if I'll know how to act being a molecule.

VANYA You should just be yourself. The molecule speaks in words, and has emotions . . . so you should not worry about what a molecule really is, and whether it can speak. But let it be a leap of faith, and just go with the flow of the words.

NINA Hmmmm, I feel this may be a crossroads for me. At this moment I can choose to be one of those actors who argues and frets and challenges endlessly, and who makes rehearsals an enormous trial. Or I can be one of those who listens and says, "All right" and just tries to make it work. I think I'll choose to become the second kind. And take a leap of faith.

VANYA Oh. What good news. Let's go out by the pond, I don't want anyone to overhear us. And you can read it aloud to me out there.

Vanya and Nina start to exit toward the outdoors.

NINA I brought my MP3 player in case you want music underneath if I read to everyone. Is that a good idea?

VANYA Oh I don't know. Maybe. Let's hear it first, and see if we should . . . ask others to . . . you know . . .

Vanya and Nina exit toward the pond.

Phone rings. Enter Cassandra from outside, carrying a few bags of groceries.

CASSANDRA I'll get it! (*answers the phone*) Hello. Who wants to know? Agnes from Country Meadows Real Estate? YOU GOT THE WRONG NUMBER, DON'T CALL HERE AGAIN!

Cassandra slams the phone down violently. Laughs and laughs. Maybe waves that Mardi Gras streamer thing around, joyously.

Sonia walks downstairs.

SONIA Goodness, who did you yell at?

CASSANDRA It was a wrong number. I got coffee and other stuff. (*Phone rings again. Cassandra looks angry, and picks up the phone.*)

CASSANDRA I TOLD YOU NOT TO CALL BACK! (*listens*) Oh, I'm sorry. I thought you were someone else. Who did you want to talk to? Well, she's right here.

Cassandra offers Sonia the phone.

SONIA Who is it?

CASSANDRA (*to phone*) Who's calling please? (*to Sonia*) Joe.

SONIA I don't know who that is.

CASSANDRA (*to phone*) She doesn't know you. (*to Sonia*) Should I hang up angry or polite?

SONIA Wait, I'll take the call. (*answers the phone*) Hello, this is Sonia. Who is this, please?

Cassandra exits with her bags off to the kitchen.

Joe? I'm afraid I don't . . . Oh yes, Joe from last night! The party, yes. What? Yes, this is Sonia. My voice sounds different? Oh. Uh.

(*thinks quickly*) Wait a minute, I have a frog in my throat. (*pretends to cough, and then switches to using her Maggie Smith voice:*) Hello, Joe. How are you today? Oh your head hurts a little. I hope you're not an alcoholic. You're not. That's good! But you like to get drunk sometimes. Well, it's a good man's failing. I'm a crack addict. No, darling . . . I'm just teasing. It was very nice to meet you last night. Remind me, what was your costume? A raincoat. Uh-huh. Anything else? A fedora. Uh-huh. So you were pretending it was raining in 1946, is that right? Oh—you were Sam Spade. The detective. I'm sorry, I should have remembered that. And Maggie Smith was actually in a movie where Peter Falk played Sam Spade, and she played Nora Charles. From *The Thin Man*. (*frowning, kind of changing her mind, still in the Maggie Smith voice*) You know, Joe, I have to go back to my own voice for a little while, do you mind? (*switches back to her normal voice*) I'm sorry, I'm a little confused. Did you really think that was my voice last night? Oh I see. Well I must have forgotten to give you the proper explanation last night. I was telling everyone I was the Evil Queen as played by Maggie Smith. But I guess by the time I met you, I had gotten tired of explaining, and you just assumed that was my real voice.

But this is my real voice, actually. It's sort of boring compared to Maggie Smith. But nonetheless, I am who I am and I'm stuck with it. I'm remembering the person who was Sam Spade. You have a very nice face. Oh I'm remembering, you said you were a widower. Is that right? I'm sorry. Two years. No, I'm not a widow. I'm a . . . (*stops for a second, chooses not to say she's never been married*) . . . I've been picky. Uh-huh. Glamorous?? (*laughs*) Oh, I must be honest and assure you I'm NOT glamorous. I look a fright most of the time. Daily, in fact. And except for last night, I've never gotten all dolled up. All right, you think of me as glamorous, I guess I should just accept it. I admit it, I'm glamorous. Do your glasses need a new prescription, Joe? They don't, all right, that's good to know. Um . . . (*thinks a second*) ... I'm a little confused. Why are you calling me today? (*listens*) Uh-huh. Uh-huh. Oh. Because you like me. How odd. What? I said, how nice.

Thank you. Although maybe it's my imitation of Maggie Smith you like. I don't do any other imitations, I'm afraid.

Uh-huh. Go to dinner? Um . . . well . . . I . . . maybe. Saturday? Well I'm not sure, let me check my book. (*She moves the phone away from her mouth and frowns; thinks; she feels nervous about saying yes, wonders what to say, makes a decision*) I'm sorry, Joe. I'm not free Saturday. Yes, it's too bad. Another time. Yes, well. Hold on a minute, would you? (*She holds the phone away, trying to think through if it makes sense to not accept this man's invitation; she's finding it very hard to make a decision; then:*) Joe. I looked at my book again, and I made a mistake. It's Sunday I'm busy. I am free Saturday. The day that you mentioned. (*he apparently took a second to take it in*) Yes, I am free. (*makes a face to herself, oh Lord, now she's said yes*) Yes, Saturday. That would be lovely. (*listens, repeats back*) Weekends are best for you. Oh—that means you have a job then. Nothing. Just I was trying to think what's the matter with you, and I couldn't come up with anything. (*as Maggie Smith*) Maybe you're mentally deficient. (*surprised at his response; goes back to her own voice*) Oh you laughed. Oh well good.

So Saturday at 6 p.m., you'll pick me up. I'm at 55 Hollyhock Road. Yes, very near where the party was. Yes, it was a nice party. Oh, and you know, if you need to cancel, I'll certainly understand. Well, all right, I just mean in case you *had* to. *No*, I would like to go. You don't mind if I don't use my Maggie Smith voice, do you? Oh that's good. I'll just use it for emphasis. Otherwise just . . . this voice. Thank you, Joe. (*a compliment*) Oh. Nice of you to say. I'll see you Saturday.

She hangs up the phone. She is extremely confused. Perhaps no one has ever asked her out before. She thinks it's maybe a joke, and she thinks it's real. She's sort of upset, and she's sort of delighted. She's afraid of expectations, and it's hard not to have some hopes.

She sits in a chair and doesn't know what she feels, but it's a mix of lots of things.

Later in the afternoon.

Vanya, Nina and Cassandra are in the Morning Room, preparing for the play reading. Cassamdra is looking at a piece of paper, reading it.

Nina has changed to a costume: she is in a diaphanous white dress, floor length, pretty, suitable for being in a Greek chorus. She may have a garland in her hair.

VANYA (*to Cassandra*)   What do you think? Are you willing to read this part of it?

CASSANDRA   Sure! Now am I a molecule or a TV weather person?

VANYA   Well you're probably a hologram actually, but why don't you ignore that and just think of yourself as a TV weather person.

CASSANDRA   All right.

VANYA   Would you turn on the music when I give you the cue?

CASSANDRA   Sure.

Masha enters, ready for the reading.

MASHA   You said 3:30. So is it time now?

VANYA   Yes, I guess it is.

MASHA (*calls off-stage*)   Spike! Sonia! Hurry up, everyone. He's ready!

Spike and Sonia come in. Sonia maybe helps Vanya move a chair or two, if needed. Masha and Spike sit on a couch together. Cassandra, holding her paper, is also seated. Sonia now sits as well.

VANYA   Thank you for coming. You're all looking at me. That's so odd. I told Nina I had written something somewhat based on the experimental play that Konstantin writes in *The Seagull*. And she read it for me today, and she wanted very much to read it aloud for you. Although I apologize. It's silly to take up your time with something that is probably no good at all.

NINA Uncle Vanya, you mustn't tell the audience that what they're about to hear is no good.

VANYA Yes, I suppose that's taking self-effacement to an unnecessary extreme.

SONIA Vanya dear, we want to hear it.

SPIKE Yeah, sounds interesting.

MASHA I have a splitting headache, but I too wish to be supportive.

VANYA Well thank you. Now I wrote it for one voice, but Nina and I conferred and we decided that certain sections should be read by other people. So just know that some of us may pop up from our seats from time to time. The setting is the universe once the earth no longer exists. Enter a molecule.

Vanya sits with the audience. A bit nervous, but serious about it all.

Sonia is seated next to Vanya.

Vanya gestures to Cassandra to push the button on the MP3 player; she does and mysterious music begins.

Nina begins.

NINA (*intones initially*)   People, lions, eagles, partridges, raccoons, porpoises, opposums. (*faster*) Hedgehogs, woodchucks, geese, spiders, octopuses. (*intoned again, or at least slower*) Foxes, wild turkeys, frogs, and blue herons.

All living creatures are dead. The earth is no more. It split apart into atoms, cells, tiny molecules.

I am one such molecule. And I am lonely.

I miss people, animals, books, oatmeal.

But they're all gone now.

The world ended sometime in the 21st century.

In the final days, it was frightening to turn on the morning weather report.

The mysterious music ends. Cassandra stands and reads from her piece of paper.

CASSANDRA Good morning, welcome to the weather. Carol Erickson couldn't be here today, so I'm filling in.
This morning Berks County is getting a tornado.
This afternoon Bucks County will have an earthquake.

This evening Berks, Bucks and Montgomery Counties will have a thunderstorm and you may find you have survived the tornado and the earthquake, but after the insane record rainfall we had in July, all the trees are going to fall over and squash your house and your car and maybe you.

And now the national forecast. Chunks of Florida fell into the ocean yesterday. It was kind of funny, except people died. Tomorrow more chunks are gonna fall into the ocean. So move to the center of the state if you can. Or hover above it all in a helicopter if you can do that.

Arizona and Texas have finished their 320th day without rain, and the entire two states are now on fire. And that's the weather.

NINA It was a horror. Horror, horror, horror. The world was like a patient who desperately needed the intensive care unit. And yet there was no intensive care to be had. Those who had pills, any pills, took them all at once and hoped to die.

Spike, who started out finding the play a pleasant distraction, is losing interest and is getting fidgety. Masha tries to get him to stop acting so antsy.

Luckily, 3 simultaneous meteorites came crashing out of the sky and put everybody out of their misery.
And just like that the earth was no more.
And what of a brother and sister who used to sit in a morning room and watch a pond out the window?

Nina motions for Vanya and Sonia to come up. They stand side by side and have typed pages with them.

VANYA Good morning, Sonia.

SONIA Good morning, Vanya.

VANYA Did you sleep well?

SONIA I don't know. Are we alive or are we dead?

VANYA We are molecules but we're remembering the past, and mourning its end.

SPIKE I don't understand this play!!!

MASHA Sssssssssh.

The people reading the play are aware of the interruption but ignore it, move on.

SONIA I remember looking out the window at the pond for years and years. Sometimes it was boring, but I miss it.

NINA I miss washing my hair.

CASSANDRA I miss ice tea. I don't like that line. I miss *Law and Order: SVU.*

SONIA I miss my self-pity. It was fun. *(gives Vanya a look, not entirely liking this line)*

NINA I miss . . . having plans for the future.

VANYA I miss boring chores which in retrospect seem wonderful. Putting the dishes away. Making a list of things to do. Licking the mail, and driving to town to . . .

SPIKE "Licking the male"! *(laughs)* That's kind of raunchy, old man.

VANYA *(a bit thrown, annoyed)* Licking the mail one is about to bring to the post office. Letters one has written. Licking the stamp that goes on the letter.

SPIKE Licking the stamp? (*doesn't understand*)

VANYA Forget it, I'll rewrite it. Maybe we should stop.

MASHA No, I like it. Keep going. (*crosses to Vanya to encourage him*) It's much better than Konstantin's play. It's more varied.

VANYA Okay. Whose line is it?

Masha is nearer to a chair by Sonia, so she sits there. She doesn't return to her seat on the couch.

NINA Mine. I miss baby powder.

VANYA I'm sorry, the "I miss" section is going on too long. Let's jump to the top of the next page.

Vanya can't return to his seat by Sonia, since Masha is in it. He is forced to sit next to Spike on the couch.

NINA All right. (*intones*) How sad to be a molecule! How sad to be a speck.

Spike's cell phone makes a small tinkle sound—a "you have a text message" sound, brief. Spike without hesitation reads the message, smiles, and starts to type a text back. He is truly unaware that it might be inappropriate to do this now. His texting goes on for a while . . . Masha gives him a signal to stop, but he holds up his finger indicating "give me a sec." Nina feels a good actress should just carry on, so she continues, and mostly pretends not to notice.

NINA How did the world come to end? Were there Cassandras we didn't listen to? Did we keep an oil burner too long?

MASHA Spike, stop that.

Spike again gestures "give me a minute," and goes back to texting.

NINA Why didn't we switch to solar panels? Why didn't we buy an electric car? Why didn't we. . . .

Vanya has had enough.

VANYA Excuse me. What are you doing? It's very rude.

SPIKE I'm still listening. I can multitask. I can drive and text, or watch a movie and tweet.

VANYA You can multitask, how wonderful. You can tweet. You twitter and tweet, you email and text, your life is abuzz with electrical communication. (*brief breath*) I know older people always think the past was better, but really—instead of a text with all these lower case letters, and no punctuation, what about a nicely crafted letter, sent through the post office? Or a thank-you note.

SPIKE Yeah, yeah, it was real elegant back then, I get it. You had to wait 5 days for a letter, but it was real nice. Time marches on, dude.

Vanya is fed up with Spike, but he's also upset about the weather, about losing the house, about his life, and about so many awful changes in the world and country. He explodes, his thoughts are almost ahead of him.

VANYA WE USED TO LICK POSTAGE STAMPS BACK THEN. Obviously you've never heard of that. They didn't just peel off ready-made with sticky stuff on the back—the sticky stuff had to be triggered by your wet tongue. It took time. If you were sending out many letters, you could be licking postage stamps for 10 minutes or so.

We used typewriters back then. And Wite-Out for corrections. And carbon paper for copies.

We had telephones and we had to dial the number by putting our index finger in a round hole representing 2 to zero. If the number was 909-9999, it could take *hours* just to dial the number. We had to have PATIENCE then. And we used to lick postage stamps. It was unpleasant, but it had to be done.

We didn't multitask. Doing one thing at a time seemed appropriate. But I guess *you* can *sort* of listen to a play and *sort* of send a message and *sort* of play a video game . . . all at once. It must be wonderful . . .

Spike is starting to get uncomfortable with Vanya's upset, and he gets up from the couch to walk away, but Vanya steps in front of him.

I know I sound like a crank, but I don't like change. My play is about scary change in the weather. But there are other changes too that have happened.

Vanya is starting to address everyone in the room, not always specifically, but sometimes. Sonia and Masha are interested by what he's saying, but also a bit concerned that he is having an outburst. Cassandra and Nina both like Vanya and pay attention, but worry a bit for him too.

There are 785 television channels. You can watch the news report that matches what you already think. In the 50s there were only 3 or 4 channels, and it was all in black-and-white.

And there were no child stars who became drug addicts like Lindsay Lohan. I mean, Hayley Mills was in the original *Parent Trap*, and she grew up to be a sensible, nice woman.

There was no *South Park*. We saw *Howdy Doody* starring a puppet. Then there was *Kukla, Fran and Ollie*—starring two more puppets, and a sweet lady named Fran. We watched puppets back then!

Sonia crosses to Vanya sympathetically and tries to get him to sit down. He is on a roll, and barely senses her; and gently encourages her to sit down instead. He doesn't stop talking, he keeps going.

There was the *Perry Como Show*. He was soothing. *The Dinah Shore Show*. She was charming.

The Bishop Sheen Show was on Sunday evening. A Catholic bishop had his own TV show. And he gave SERMONS. On TV. We weren't Catholic, but we watched him anyway. He said sensible things. On television.

The Ed Sullivan Show was on before *Bishop Sheen,* and he had opera singers on, And performers from current Broadway shows. Richard Burton and Julie Andrews would sing songs from *Camelot.* It was wonderful. It helped theater be part of the national consciousness, which it isn't anymore.

And he had Señor Wences on, who had a Spanish accent and was a ventriloquist. And he painted a mouth on his fist, and he would make it speak.

He speaks in funny voice—high one, very low one, high one—and uses his hand and thumb to imitate the way Señor Wences used his hand as a speaking puppet.

(*high*) "Hello," (*low*) "Hello," (*high*) "Hello." (*low*) Hello. His act lasted about . . . seven hours. As a child I thought to myself, this must be what eternity feels like. And yet that's a good concept for a child to have.

SPIKE I thought you were talking about things you liked in the past.

VANYA You're right. I'm inconsistent. I don't know what I'm saying. Be quiet. BE QUIET.

We licked postage stamps, and we sent letters.

I preferred Bishop Sheen to Señor Wences. Bishop Sheen was a good speaker, and he used his real mouth rather than one drawn onto his fist, and this made me take him more seriously.

I remember him talking about the seed falling on the good soil, falling on the bad soil, the seed falling on rock. In other words, build your life on a strong foundation.

Of course, I haven't done that. But I meant to. Bishop Sheen said I should. I guess I got lost. But it was interesting to hear him talk that way. It was *articulate*. I don't think much is articulate in the world anymore.

And I'm saying this all in retrospect. I didn't think it when I was 10. I was just trying to get through life one day at a time when I was 10.

(*to Spike*) And I didn't have a life ahead of me where I was going to be almost cast in *Entourage 2*. But I guess you're having a good life, and I had foolish one.

Tell me, do they have any older characters on *Entourage 2*? Do they need someone in their late 50s, who has had a useless life and is looking back feeling bitter? Might I audition for that part? Could you check?

Masha is worried about Vanya. She crosses to him.

80

MASHA Vanya, darling, you seem overwrought, and you're talking way more than usual. Do you not want to go lie down somewhere?

VANYA I have the remainder of my life to nap. I'm not done yet. WE LICKED POSTAGE STAMPS! We didn't have answering machines. You had to call people back. (*Masha moves away.*) We ate Spam, just like the soldiers in World War II did. (*to Spike*) Have you *heard* of World War II?

We played Scrabble and Monopoly. We didn't play video games, in some virtual reality, where we would kill policemen and prostitutes as if that was some sort of entertainment.

The popular entertainment wasn't so insane back then. It was sometimes corny, but sincere. We all saw the movie *Davy Crockett* and wore coonskin caps.

That may not sound sane, wearing those caps, but it was very innocent. And we *all* did it, there was a solidarity about it, unlike being alone in your room killing prostitutes in a video game.

We followed *The Adventures of Ozzie and Harriet.* Which starred the real life Ozzie and Harriet Nelson.

But *Adventures* was a strange word for the show because it was *extremely* uneventful. They did things like . . . make popcorn in the kitchen. Or . . . look for missing socks.

In retrospect they seemed medicated.

It was a stupid show, but it was calming. You didn't feel it was stirring people up and creating serial killers.

I'm sorry I'm getting off the point. But my point is the 50s were idiotic but I miss parts of them. When I was 13 I saw *Goldfinger* with Sean Connery as James Bond, and I didn't get the meaning of the character name of "Pussy Galore." Went right over my head.

Nowadays, three-year-olds get the joke. They can barely walk and they know what Pussy Galore means.

The weather is changing, the culture is very weird. I'm not a conservative, but I do miss things in the past.

I Love Lucy was pretty wonderful. And the whole country watched it. We saw *Davy Crockett.* And *The Mickey Mouse Show.* Boys just past puberty would fixate on Annette Funicello.

81

We didn't identify with rock stars, we identified with Mouseketeers. Annette, Darlene Gillespie, Cubby O'Brien.

My favorite was Tommy Kirk who was one of the Hardy Boys on the Mickey Mouse show. Later he starred in Disney's *Old Yeller*, about a boy and his dog. His father was fighting in the Civil War, but Tommy was the one who took the responsibility for being the grown-up. Not his mother or younger brother.

And initially he didn't want the dog, but then he bonded with it. And at the end of the film Old Yeller gets rabies and foams at the mouth, and poor Tommy Kirk has to shoot his dog, crying his eyes out as he does so.

It was a traumatic moment in our national past. A shared one.

I wondered what happened to Tommy Kirk, and I did a Google search and I learned that sometime after he was in *Son of Flubber*, Walt Disney found out that Tommy Kirk was gay and he fired him. He dropped his contract.

Meanwhile Tab Hunter was gay too, but HIS studio just saw to it that he went on pretend dates with starlets. They didn't fire Tab Hunter. They starred him in movies opposite Sophia Loren, for God's sake. Tommy Kirk on the other hand was mistreated, and I TAKE IT PERSONALLY. As I expect he does too.

He stopped making movies. He took drugs for a period. And then later he got better and became a minister. And now he runs a rug cleaning business. I guess he's all right.

But he's had to go through the same changes I have—no more licking of postage stamps, no more typewriters or letters, no more shared national TV shows like *Ozzie and Harriet* which even though it was boring still it was a SHARED MEMORY BETWEEN US. There are no shared memories anymore.

Now, now there's twitter and email and Facebook and cable and satellite, and the movies and TV shows are all worthless, and we don't even watch the same worthless things together, it's all separate. And our lives are . . . disconnected.

And you come in here and say you almost had a part on *Entourage 2* as if that's an achievement of some kind. And I don't know what you're talking about.

I'm worried about the future. I miss the past. I don't want to talk anymore. I'm going to go sit in the other room. I don't know why I exploded. Sorry. (*exits*)

SPIKE Wow, what's up with him? That was a major flip out.

SONIA I think I better go after him.

NINA Can I come?

Sonia and Nina exit after Vanya.

SPIKE You come from a crazy family.

MASHA You come from a family who taught you no manners. Why did you find it necessary to text during Vanya's play?

SPIKE Well he didn't have to go nuts about it.

MASHA (*takes his phone out of his hand*) What were you texting, for God's sake? (*reads*) "I'll meet you at the airport 8 a.m. Tuesday. Love you."

SPIKE It's my cousin. I'm bringing her to the airport.

MASHA How thoughtful. And usually you're never thoughtful. I recognize the screen name you're writing to. HootiePie at gmail.com

CASSANDRA Beware of Hootie Pie.

MASHA I didn't realize Hootie Pie was your cousin.

SPIKE She's not. Hootie Pie and I . . . are in love.

MASHA In love? With my personal assistant?

CASSANDRA And Hootie Pie shall be called Spawn of the Devil.

SPIKE Does she have to stay here?

MASHA Suddenly I like her.

CASSANDRA Thank you. Suddenly I like you.

SPIKE All right then. On Tuesday morning Hootie and I will be flying to Aruba for two weeks. And then we're renting an apartment together. I was going to tell you on Monday.

MASHA Well you've told me today. Cassandra, please call a taxi for Spike. I want him to get on an uncomfortable bus and go back to New York and be out of my life.

SPIKE I was gonna tell you. I didn't want to ruin your weekend.

MASHA Well that's just so thoughtful of you, thank you. And how good to know how loyal and helpful Hootie/Spawn of the Devil has been. Was she ever going to tell me she was quitting?

SPIKE She was going to send you an email.

MASHA An email. How classy.

SPIKE She was afraid to tell you in person.

MASHA You know, she doesn't need to be. I find myself feeling sudden and enormous relief about having you out of my life, and Hootie Pie too. (*noticing Cassandra is still here*) Cassandra, did you call the taxi?

CASSANDRA We don't have a taxi in town.

MASHA Well . . . can you solve it?

CASSANDRA I can drive him myself.

MASHA Good. I'm liking you more and more.

CASSANDRA And vice versa. Ms. Hardwicke, I want to apologize for something.

MASHA What?

CASSANDRA (*pause*) I don't want to say, but I just want to apologize.

MASHA I appreciate it. Thank you very much. (*turns back to Spike*) Goodbye, Spike. It was fun, sort of, have a good life, I've been a fool, so long. Now please go get your things and go with Cassandra and be banished to a bus.

SPIKE I'm sorry if I hurt you.

MASHA I'm sorry if you hurt me too. But you may not have. I notice my headache is gone.

SPIKE May I kiss you?

MASHA No.

SPIKE . . . May I shake hands?

MASHA Yes. (*They shake hands.*) I wish you success.

SPIKE Thank you.

Spike exits up to the bedroom.

CASSANDRA (*said simply, marveling in retrospect how correct her warning has been*) Beware of Hootie Pie.

MASHA Indeed.

Phone rings. Masha picks up.

MASHA (*into the phone*) Hello? Who? Oh, Agnes. (*whispers to Cassandra*) It's that woman about the house. (*back to the phone*) YOU GOT THE WRONG NUMBER, DON'T CALL HERE AGAIN! (*hangs up*)

CASSANDRA That's exactly what I said earlier today.

MASHA We are clearly sharing some psychic connection. And I welcome it. (*calls off-stage*) Vanya, Sonia! Come in here please!

Vanya and Sonia enter, followed by Nina.

MASHA I am not selling the house. Hootie Pie is a manipulator and a liar, and she was wrong about the Snow White costume, and clearly all her other suggestions are wrong too. So in no way will I consider the suggestion she made that I sell the house.

SONIA What happened?

MASHA Cassandra is driving Spike to the bus, he's out of my life, he's running off with Hootie Pie.

SONIA Oh. I'm sorry.

MASHA Don't be. I'm feeling very good . . . except for the fact I have such very bad taste in men. And I don't know why I wanted to sell the house. Oh, I have less money than I used to. And I was going to turn down this film where they want me to play a grandmother, which I am not anxious to do. But I think I'll take it for the money. It would pay the mortgage for like a year. You know, I don't know why I didn't think this earlier, but I don't have a husband, I don't have children . . . but the roots I do have are here, aren't they? With you two.

Vanya and Sonia give Masha a hug. She hugs back. They hold it for a bit, then separate.

CASSANDRA Uh-oh. Lover boy's coming down the stairs.

Spike comes down the stairs. He looks good, is carrying a small overnight bag. Everyone is kind of uncomfortable. Spike does not seem uncomfortable.

SPIKE *(friendly, nice, as if nothing's happened)* Thank you all for a lovely weekend. I enjoyed meeting all of you.

SONIA Yes, it was lovely. We all had a great time. *(she looks at everyone else, making a "is he crazy or what" face)*

VANYA I'm sorry about my tirade. I didn't mean to go ballistic.

SPIKE That's okay. Always good to get things out. Thank you, Masha, it was great getting to know you.

MASHA Yes, lovely to meet you. You must send me photos of you and Hootie Pie cavorting in Aruba.

SPIKE Really?

MASHA Yes. I'll put them on the refrigerator with all the coupons.

SPIKE So long, Nina.

NINA Goodbye, Spike.

CASSANDRA Come on, Spike-y. Let's head to the bus.

SPIKE Spike.

Spike gives a little wave to them, and exits with Cassandra. A brief bit of silence.

MASHA I think I need to take a walk by the pond, and digest the entirety of the last 15 minutes. And maybe the last 15 years. I think I mostly feel happy, but I can't figure out why. Oh, and Vanya—I LOVED your play, although you did upstage it with your harangue at Spike, which I also loved.

VANYA Oh, thanks. And Nina was very good.

MASHA Yes, she was.

NINA Oh thank you. Was I? I know I stood up straight and spoke loudly, but wasn't sure I entirely inhabited being a molecule.

MASHA Oh, writers ask you to play such difficult things. I thought you were very good as a molecule, rather ethereal, which I always had hoped molecules would be.

NINA Really? How wonderful.

MASHA Now let me go take my walk, and evaluate my life. (*exits to the grass, and the pond*)

VANYA You know, Sonia—we've got to get jobs. We can't expect her to keep sending us a monthly stipend, when we just sit home doing nothing. How much is minimum wage, does anyone know?

NINA I think it's $7 and some change.

SONIA Work. Really? Who would ever hire us?

VANYA That unfortunately is a good question.

NINA I saw a help wanted sign at CVS Pharmacy.

SONIA Oh God. I'd prefer death.

NINA Oh, I'm sorry, I thought you wanted a job.

SONIA No, Vanya thought I should have a job. I think I should have a cocktail.

VANYA Well, we'll have to keep talking about it. There may be things we can do . . .

SONIA Oh I'm sure they'll pay us 15 cents.

VANYA Sonia, you're right, it'll be really difficult and maybe awful. But if Masha has the generosity to continue paying for this house, we have to earn something to contribute to our living expenses.

SONIA Oh dear. Well maybe I'll marry Joe and he'll end up being really wealthy.

VANYA What? Who?

SONIA I got a phone call. Someone from the party. Asked me to dinner. His name is Joe. Of course, it's just dinner . . . I'm sure he won't like me, but if he does like me, oh I'd so prefer that to CVS Pharmacy.

VANYA Well that's great that someone called you.

SONIA I know. I never meet anyone, I don't think I've been to a party in 20 years. It's encouraging but of course I mustn't get my hopes up.

NINA You must always get your hopes up.

SONIA Really? That sounds wise but scary.

NINA I have so loved meeting you both. Dear Sonia, dear Uncle Vanya. I am going to come out to visit my aunt and uncle more often, so I can see you both.

Nina hugs them both, exits.

VANYA She's very sweet. I like her.

SONIA Yes, she is nice. Although I can only stand a little bit of people wondering how to play a molecule.

VANYA Oh look, she forgot her music playing thing. (*picks it up, music starts to play*) Oh I turned it on. How do you turn it off?

The music is the Beatles' "Here Comes the Sun."

SONIA Don't turn it off. It's nice. The Beatles.

VANYA Nina has such surprising taste. Foreign movies, the Beatles. She may be living in a time warp.

Masha reenters.

MASHA I'm back. My dark night of the soul was very brief, and I got lonely. What are you two doing?

SONIA We're listening to music.

VANYA Nina left her music thing.

MASHA Oh, the Beatles, nice.

SONIA Let's sit and wait for the blue heron to come.

VANYA It usually comes in the morning.

SONIA I think it'll come late afternoon today. To celebrate.

VANYA Well we can hope.

SONIA Always hope.

VANYA And if it doesn't come this afternoon, I'm almost positive it'll be back in the morning.

Slight pause.

MASHA What a day. "Oh, Olga, let's go to Moscow."

SONIA I don't want to go to Moscow. (*pause*) I like it here.

They all three stare out the window. Their bodies start to move, idiosyncratically but in rhythm, with the music. Lights dim. End of play.